BALDWIN LOCOMOTIVES

BRIAN SOLOMON

Voyageur Press

To Kurt Bell, whose dedication to the preservation
of railway history has made this book possible.

First published in 2010 by MBI Publishing Company and Voyageur Press, an imprint of MBI Publishing Company, 400 First Avenue North, Suite 300, Minneapolis, MN 55401 USA

The information in this book is true and complete to the best of our knowledge. All recommendations are made without any guarantee on the part of the author or Publisher, who also disclaims any liability incurred in connection with the use of this data or specific details.

We recognize, further, that some words, model names, and designations mentioned herein are the property of the trademark holder. We use them for identification purposes only. This is not an official publication.

Voyageur Press titles are also available at discounts in bulk quantity for industrial or sales-promotional use. For details write to Special Sales Manager at MBI Publishing Company, 400 First Avenue North, Suite 300, Minneapolis, MN 55401 USA.

To find out more about our books, visit us online at www.voyageurpress.com.

Library of Congress Cataloging-in-Publication Data

Solomon, Brian, 1966-
  Baldwin locomotives / Brian Solomon. — 1st ed.
     p. cm.
  Includes bibliographical references and index.
  ISBN 978-0-7603-3589-5 (hb w/ jkt)
  1. Baldwin locomotives. 2. Baldwin Locomotive Works—History. 3. Locomotives—United States—History. I. Title.

TJ625.B2S65 2010
625.260973—dc22
                    2009028542

Front cover: Baldwin began building road diesels for heavy service in the mid-1940s. These Baltimore & Ohio DF-8s were builder's model RF16s that used the distinctive Baldwin carbody style commonly known as the sharknose. They were photographed working in mineral service during spring 1951 shortly after delivery from Baldwin-Lima-Hamilton. *H. L. Broadbelt Baldwin Collection (RR88.2), Railroad Museum of Pennsylvania (PHMC)*

Frontis: This frontal view of Chesapeake & Ohio 1572 characterizes the appearance of the railroad's late-era steam. *Baldwin image No. 9713, construction No. 58964, courtesy H. L. Broadbelt Baldwin Collection (RR88.2), Railroad Museum of Pennsylvania (PHMC)*

Title pages: This posed publicity photo was made on 8x10 black-and-white sheet film. It shows a set of new Pennsylvania Railroad RF-16 sharks with a westward freight passing Banks Tower, located at the far western end of the Philadelphia Division along the west bank of the Susquehanna River west of Marysville. *Baldwin image No. 16313, courtesy H. L. Broadbelt Baldwin Collection (RR88.2), Railroad Museum of Pennsylvania (PHMC)*

Contents page: Nevada short line Virginia & Truckee Railroad's first locomotive was this unusual 2-4-0 bought from Baldwin in 1875. V&T's No. 21, *J. W. Bowker*, is a beautiful little locomotive. Remarkably, it survives today, preserved at the California State Railroad Museum in Sacramento, California. *Baldwin image No. 90, construction No. 3689, courtesy H. L. Broadbelt Baldwin Collection (RR88.2), Railroad Museum of Pennsylvania (PHMC)*

Back cover: Rear view of the firebox on a Pennsylvania Railroad T1 exposed on January 29, 1942. *Baldwin image No. 12160-42, courtesy H. L. Broadbelt Baldwin Collection (RR88.2), Railroad Museum of Pennsylvania (PHMC)*

Editor: Dennis Pernu
Design Manager: LeAnn Kuhlmann
Designer: Lois Stanfield
Jacket Designer: Simon Larkin

CONTENTS

ACKNOWLEDGMENTS

IN THE PROCESS OF ASSEMBLING THIS BOOK, I have had help from a number of people, all of whom deserve applause for their efforts. The staff at the Railroad Museum of Pennsylvania went the extra mile to help me with this project over the course of many visits. First and foremost is Kurt Bell, the museum's archivist, who not only inspired me take on this project but helped me navigate the museum's archives and locate many treasures, some of which probably had not been exposed to light in decades. Kurt's personal interest in this project made it a pleasure to undertake. Kurt also lent me his writings and perspectives on the Broadbelt Collection, as well as information on various key Baldwin figures, such as Paul T. Warner, Frederick Westing, and Samuel M. Vauclain.

Also crucial were the efforts of the museum's Nicholas Zmijewski, who spent many hours scanning Baldwin negatives, photographs, and various other artifacts. Nick's sharp memory for details saved me hours of retracing my steps, especially when I needed to re-inspect specific plates for data. Although it may not be apparent, only a very small portion of the surviving Baldwin photographic collection is presented here. I personally sifted through an estimated 10,000 images. Nick has gone through virtually every relevant image relating to the project; his ability to navigate the files is a special asset to the museum and anyone doing research there.

Thanks to John Gruber of the Center for Railroad Photography and Art for proofreading the sidebars, tracing dates, and offering ideas and perspective. My father, Richard Jay Solomon, lent me use of his vast library and photo collection, helped with scanning, and provided copyediting of original drafts. My brother, Seán Solomon, and Isabelle Dijols provided lodging in Philadelphia. Seán also accompanied me on a walking tour of the former site of Baldwin's Broad and Spring Garden Streets plant in downtown Philadelphia—after an hour of searching, we concluded that there are few traces of Baldwin's once important locomotive plant, although there is more to see at its newer, although long-closed, former Eddystone facilities. Thanks to my mother, Maureen, for helping with travel logistics and bookkeeping.

The Irish Railway Record Society in Dublin granted me unrestricted access to their archives. Frank Tatnall, Samuel M. Vauclain's great-grandson, assisted with details about the Vauclain family. Robert A. Buck of Tucker's Hobbies in Warren, Massachusetts, shared with me many of his experiences watching Baldwins at work, as well as memories of Baldwin's Charles A. Brown. I met Charlie only once and had little idea that I would someday write a book on his former employer. Thanks to Patrick Yough for helping me to track down details. Kevin Kohls provided perspective on the Broadbelt Collection and details on the company photographers. Tim Doherty lent me copies of *Baldwin Locomotives* magazine. Philip A. Brahms lent me some photographs of a Baldwin diesel at work in California.

In my research and writing I've consulted a vast array of sources. A nearly complete listing can be found in the bibliography. Over the years, several very informative books have been written about Baldwin locomotives and the company's business. I regularly consulted various Baldwin Locomotive Works company histories and Frederick Westing's *The Locomotives That Baldwin Built*. *Diesels from Eddystone: The Story of Baldwin Diesel Locomotives* by Gary W. Dolzall and Stephen F. Dolzall, and John Kirkland's *The Diesel Builder Series* and *Dawn of the*

Diesel Age provide comprehensive overviews of the company's foray into dieseldom. John K. Brown's *The Baldwin Locomotive Works 1831–1915* provides an excellent understanding of Baldwin's business and methods in the golden age of steam. *The Steam Locomotive in America* by Alfred W. Bruce, *The American Steam Locomotive: Volume 1, Evolution* by Frank M. Swengel, and John H. White Jr.'s various works on nineteenth-century steam helped put Baldwin's steam production in perspective. For locomotive details, performance, and dates, I mined various railroad trade magazines, including Angus Sinclair's *Railroad and Locomotive Engineering*, *Railroad Mechanical Engineer*, *Diesel Railway Traction*, and *Railway Age*. In addition, I went through a vast array of Baldwin's published data, as well as company documents, letters, and locomotive registers.

Among the interesting, and occasionally frustrating, elements of my research was reconciling incongruities in Baldwin data, dates, and statistics while trying to track down missing information. This might come as a shock to some purists, but within Baldwin's own company records I found errors and discrepancies. If Baldwin's engineers and clerks couldn't keep the numbers straight on all of the 70,000 plus locomotives built, it would seem certain that further confusion occurred once locomotives left the factory. In some cases, locomotives were ordered, built, and lettered for one railroad and then photographed, only to be sold to another line. For some locomotives, various sources have reported different specifications, and I found considerable variance in reported locomotive weights. In some situations, this was because a prototype would have technical variations from later production versions; in others, owning railroads would report a different weight than the weight Baldwin offered in its literature. In the case of Pennsylvania Railroad's Class I1s, I found no less than three different reported figures for "total engine weight." On each locomotive profiled I chose the data that I believed to be most accurate, which most often came from statistics originating at Baldwin. I've tried to ensure a high level of accuracy, however, if I have made mistakes, future authors can delight in correcting them, for this book is by no means the last word on Baldwin.

Of the thousands of Baldwin company photographs, most depict locomotives long since sent to scrap, so it was a bit of a thrill to locate a builder's image of East Broad Top No. 15 (below) and then two days later travel to photograph it under steam (top). On June 7, 2009, No. 15 led an excursion from Colgate Grove to Orbisonia, Pennsylvania. Ninety-five years after it left Baldwin, this three-foot-gauge Mikado still works a portion of the line for which it was built. In 1956, the same year Baldwin ended locomotive production, East Broad Top shut down as a common carrier. The line was bought by a scrapper, who, rather than salvaging the property, preserved both the railroad and its locomotives. *Author photo; Baldwin image No. 4285, construction No. 41196, courtesy H. L. Broadbelt Baldwin Collection (RR88.2), Railroad Museum of Pennsylvania (PHMC)*

Special thanks to my editor Dennis Pernu and everyone at Voyageur Press for taking the time to take my text, specification bars, scanned photo files, and color slides and transform them into a book. It might seem strange, but the book you now hold in your hands is for me, as I write this, purely a conceptual item.

Built in 1899, Western New York & Pennsylvania's 2-8-0 No. 177 featured a Belpaire firebox. This railroad operated a network of lines across its namesake territory and later amalgamated into the Pennsylvania Railroad system. At the time of this photograph, the Consolidation type was a standard heavy freight locomotive on many lines across North America. *Baldwin image No. 1240, construction No. 17120, courtesy H. L. Broadbelt Baldwin Collection (RR88.2), Railroad Museum of Pennsylvania (PHMC)*

INTRODUCTION

Opposite: In 1942, Baldwin built a pair of experimental streamlined Duplexes for Pennsylvania Railroad. Baldwin documented various stages of construction. In this view exposed on January 21, 1941, a PRR T1 prototype is lifted inside the Eddystone plant. *Baldwin image No. 12160-36, courtesy H. L. Broadbelt Baldwin Collection (RR88.2), Railroad Museum of Pennsylvania (PHMC)*

IN THE FORMATIVE DAYS of American railroading, the Baldwin Locomotive Works emerged as a leading builder of railroad steam locomotives. By the mid-nineteenth century, it was well established as the foremost name in locomotive construction. By the early twentieth century, it was constructing more than 2,000 locomotives a year and selling its machines to railways around the world. Baldwin built established types and innovated new designs, and produced locomotives drafted by its customers. It was known and respected for its high-quality products. Baldwin was not limited to steam, and from the end of the nineteenth century it contributed the mechanical portions of electric locomotives jointly manufactured with Westinghouse.

Although the company was a pioneer of diesel-electric technology, Baldwin's predominance faltered as diesel technology matured. In the 1930s, Baldwin's competitors developed and refined diesel locomotives that undermined its once lucrative steam locomotive business. Although Baldwin developed a full line of diesels in the 1940s, the company was unable to keep pace with demands on its technology, and in 1956, following a sharp decline in its market share, it ended domestic locomotive production. By that time it had produced more than 70,500 locomotives for domestic and international applications.

Since its early days, Baldwin sought to render illustrations of its locomotives, both for the company's detailed records and to

help promote its designs to prospective buyers. Yet, Baldwin's locomotive business predated the advent of practical commercial photography, and in its first decades locomotives were illustrated by traditional means. Although it would be considered difficult to use by today's standards, the wet collodion process developed by Frederick Scott Archer in 1851 was a significant step forward in photography. This required a photographer to mix photosensitive chemicals in a darkened room, coat polished glass plates with a chemical solution, and sensitize them with the freshly mixed photochemistry. The plate was exposed while still wet—thus the common term "wet-plate photography"—and processed in the dark immediately after exposure. Wet-plate photography produced a superior image and was faster and easier than most earlier processes. More importantly, it allowed for a very sharp negative image that could be easily copied by printing on photosensitized albumen paper.

By 1859, further improvements in the wet collodion process had advanced to the point where Baldwin was able to commission photographers routinely to make images of new locomotives. Railroad Museum of Pennsylvania archivist and historian Kurt Bell has written that many of the earliest surviving Baldwin builder images are believed to be the work of Coleman Sellers, a Philadelphia-based photographer working in the then-popular stereo card medium. It had become a standard practice in the locomotive industry to document the completion of significant locomotive types. Bell writes that in the 1860s, Baldwin switched from the common stereo-card format to large-format horizontal portraits of its finished locomotives. Only a scant few images from this period have survived. A handful of these, some of which are included in this book, appear in the personal notebook kept by Baldwin partner George Burnham, who in the 1860s kept details of selected locomotives for his own use. The notebook is now preserved in the museum's archives.

According to Bell, by late 1870 Baldwin had discontinued the practice of hiring outside photographers and established its own photography program, complete with staff photographers and a processing laboratory. This program continued until 1954, and the bulk of the locomotive portraits, as well as many other views in this book, are products of these efforts. Not all of Baldwin's photographic staff is known, but it is believed that Harrison Tyron served as Baldwin's photographer from about 1880 to about 1920, and after that Fred Haines worked as the company photographer until 1954 when the in-house program was disbanded. Other late-era members of Baldwin's photographic staff included assistant photographer Gerhard R. Reese, Florence McIntyre, and Doris Hoffner. Kevin Kohls, Baldwin Locomotive Works photo historian, explained in interviews that the late-era color images of Baldwin's Mechydro diesels were made under contract with New York photographer Jules Schick. He also noted that Tyron may have been a contract photographer.

Virtually every company photograph was documented and logged in a detailed register. Each image was assigned a number, which began with 1 and continued more or less sequentially through the 17,000 series. As Bell emphasizes, Baldwin did not photograph every locomotive it built and often only made images of representative locomotives of a certain type, or of very unusual machines. Although images were catalogued and stored in numerical order, and the number series tends to progress chronologically, locomotives portrayed were not necessarily built in the order photographed. Many of the earliest images appear to have been assigned numbers retroactively, and the build dates visible on locomotive builder's plates indicate large gaps in the plates logged in Baldwin's official register. It is likely that many of the earliest images were lost or destroyed prior to Baldwin's establishment of its numbering system.

Other incongruities disrupt the chronology as well. Often, locomotives that had been built over a period of weeks or months were held back and photographed over the course of a day or two. It appears that little effort was made to photograph these locomotives in the specific order of construction. Chronological discrepancies were sometimes caused by a lag between the time when a builder's plate was attached and the date a locomotive was posed for its portrait. In other situations, Baldwin's photographers recopied old images, so a copy photograph of an image portraying a locomotive built in the 1860s

Raymond Loewy's elegant styling added an element of sophistication to Baldwin's high-speed Duplex. This 4x5-inch Kodachrome was exposed on a photographer's publicity run in 1942 on the railroad's famed Rockville Bridge over the Susquehanna. PRR No. 6111 was one of two T1 prototypes built during World War II. After the war, PRR ordered 50 production T1s that ran for a few years in fast passenger service but were soon replaced by diesels. *Courtesy Matt Gray Collection (RR95.2), Railroad Museum of Pennsylvania (PHMC)*

will bear a sequential number reflecting the time of copying rather than when original image was made.

The vast majority of images were made in the time-established tradition of builder's photographs: namely, a well-lit broadside depicting a finished locomotive prior to shipping. By the 1870s, it became a common technique either to photograph the engine in front of a white sheet or, as was standard practice for many years, alter the negative with an opaquing solution to present the locomotive against a white background in the final print. Builder's photographs were typically printed and retained on file

Southern Pacific cab-forward Class AC-7 No. 4153 was photographed at Eddystone in 1937. This was one of many classes of massive, oil-burning, cab-forward steam locomotives that Baldwin built for SP mainline mountain service. Unlike the early cab-forward types, this later machine uses a simple-articulated design with high pressure to all cylinders. *Baldwin image No. 15272, courtesy H. L. Broadbelt Baldwin Collection (RR88.2), Railroad Museum of Pennsylvania (PHMC)*

1786

Baldwin built many small locomotives for industrial applications. Compressed-air engines like Pennsylvania Coal Company No. 6 were designed for specialized situations, such as mining, where coal-fired steam locomotives would have been unsuitable. *Baldwin image No. 1732, construction No. 23447, courtesy H. L. Broadbelt Baldwin Collection (RR88.2), Railroad Museum of Pennsylvania (PHMC)*

for distribution. Many builder's images were printed on specification cards that featured key mechanical data on the back along with the Baldwin locomotive class, negative number, and other relevant details particular to the locomotive. Another element of the official portrait was a special application of flat paint. Kohls notes that in the 1930s or 1940s this cost about $90 per side of the locomotive. When this practice began is not clear, and it was not applied in every situation.

In addition to the common opaqued broadside views, Baldwin photographers occasionally made images from other angles. Some locomotives were posed in three-quarter views—an angle adopted years later by amateur photographers as the now common "roster shot." If a locomotive had an unusual front end, a head-on architectural-type portrait might be made where the front of the smokebox was on an even plane with the film emulsion. (Baldwin's photographers worked with large-format-view cameras that had a variety of adjustments enabling them to control perspective.) After 1900, photographers occasionally made large-format action photos of Baldwin locomotives at work. They also photographed locomotives under construction and produced detail images of key components. On some occasions, they photographed plant managers, company officials, visiting dignitaries, and other key people with locomotives on company grounds and at company events. Sometimes photographs made by photographers from the railroads were sent and copied for addition into the Baldwin archive. Thus, not all images in the Baldwin negative file are of Baldwin locomotives, which occasionally results in confusion.

Over the years, Baldwin photographers kept pace with changes in the medium. The transition from collodion wet plates to commercially produced "dry plates" appears to have occurred after image No. 250 was exposed (circa 1885?). This transition has caused some confusion because some historians have casually assumed that all glass negatives were wet plates, when in fact most were not. Only a small portion of the surviving Baldwin glass negatives were exposed using the wet collodion process. Most of the plates, wet and dry, were exposed in various established formats over the years, including 15x29, 9x16, 8x10, and 4x7, typically in the landscape perspective. Another transition occurred during the second decade of the twentieth century, when Baldwin switched from commercial dry plates to 7x11 and 12x20 nitrate-based sheet film. Later, according to Kohls, it adopted Dupont Defender sheet film. This stable media overcame inherent deficiencies of the nitrate base. Although film was easier to work with, the flexible nature of the film base did not always yield uniformly sharp results from corner to corner, especially in the larger sizes.

Black-and-white photography dominates the Railroad Museum of Pennsylvania's Baldwin collection. While the Kodachrome transparency process was introduced commercially in 1935, Baldwin did not begin using color until about 1939. Kohls cites a photo of Missouri Pacific VO 1000 No. 9103 (builder No. 62301) shipped November 3, 1939, as its earliest known Kodachrome. Baldwin worked with various sizes of large-format Kodachrome. Among the few steam locomotives exposed in color were the two T1 Duplex prototypes built for Pennsylvania Railroad. Other Kodachrome images were made of the early road-diesel prototypes. While Baldwin

photographers continued to expose some black-and-white images, color photography became standard after World War II and tended to coincide with Baldwin's emphasis on diesel-electric production. Most of the later color images were made using large-format Anscochrome where two photos (usually an exposure bracket of the same locomotive) were made on one sheet.

Considering their age, many of the Baldwin negatives have survived remarkably well, but others have not. Glass negatives, while offering a phenomenally sharp original, are prone to fracture when dropped or handled roughly. A fair number of Baldwin plates have cracked or shattered over the years. Furthermore, a great many of the earliest images are missing. Nor have changes in photographic processes always benefited longevity. Some of the processes have held up better than others. In some instances, the opaquing material has reacted with the photographic emulsion, resulting in badly deteriorated images. The nitrate base used in early sheet film is inherently unstable, and many of these images have suffered. Ironically, many of the most recent images—those of the Baldwin diesels—have deteriorated as a result of unstable color dyes and less-than-ideal storage practices. While the Kodachromes from the mid-1940s have held up very well, since these dyes were relatively stable, the Anscochromes have faded badly, and many of the surviving color transparencies display a pronounced color shift as a result of dyes fading at different rates.

Most of the surviving Baldwin locomotive negatives are part of the museum's Broadbelt Collection. In the 1950s, Herbert L. Broadbelt, a draftsman at Baldwin with a passion for locomotives, saved these priceless images from oblivion. For 30 years after Baldwin ceased production, Broadbelt ran a business out of his home selling copies of Baldwin locomotive photos to enthusiasts. The Friends of the Railroad Museum of Pennsylvania bought the collection from Broadbelt in 1986 and 1987, and it was delivered in 1988. The museum has spent 20 years archiving and preserving it for future generations. Most recently, this has included the daunting tasks of digitally scanning the images and photographically copying older plates onto film. (In addition, some builder's photos were preserved by Matt Gray and have since joined the museum's original collection.)

Also drawn upon for this book are a wealth of other Baldwin materials and images in the museum's archives, including a vast collection of photo specification cards (many from the W. A. Lucas and T. T. Taber collections), company publications, Baldwin nineteenth-century dry-mounted prints, and personal collections, such as those from long-time Baldwin librarian and historian Paul T. Warner.

MAKING THE SELECTIONS

I could easily produce a half-dozen volumes like this on Baldwin locomotives and never risk printing the same image twice. Working with the museum's Kurt Bell and Nicholas Zmijewski, I pared down a manageable selection of 600 images from more than 15,000 surviving Baldwin builder's photos and other materials. Working from this, I refined it to the 160–180 images printed in this book. My intent has been to illustrate a history of Baldwin locomotives using the company photos and archives. Although many Baldwin photos have been published over the years, I found images in the archives that I had never seen before. I've augmented the official Baldwin photographs with other materials from the Baldwin archives and included a variety of images to break up the monotony of the standard builder's angle.

Although this book is *a* history of Baldwin, I do not pretend to offer it as *the* history. My text spans the gamut of Baldwin locomotive production and features many of the more interesting, technologically significant, or unusual machines built by the Baldwin Locomotive Works—this is not intended to be a comprehensive company history. I've distilled the story of locomotive development while paying close attention to technological innovation and changes in the railroad industry and locomotive marketplace. I've considered chronological development of the different engine types in each chapter, yet there is considerable chronological overlap between chapters. I focused one chapter on compound locomotives built between 1889 and 1926. Provided sufficient space and time, I could have done the same for other locomotive categories, including engines built for industrial applications, transit services, export, or specialized service. Certainly whole books could be written on Southern Pacific's cab-forward articulateds and Pennsylvania T1 Duplexes, both of which are also special interests of mine.

Locomotive devotees may wonder why certain notable or famous locomotives have not been pictured. This is due partly to space limitations, but it is also because, rather than simply focus on Baldwin's hit parade, I hoped to emphasize some more obscure images, perhaps never before published. Specifically, I selected images that I found the most interesting. I hope that you, too, find the images interesting, but that you also find the text illuminating and enjoy learning about Baldwin's locomotives as much as I have.

First in Baldwin's photo register is image 00001, made on October 25, 1871, of New York & Oswego Midland's 2-6-0 *Franklin* No. 33. This image is from a print, since the original glass plate has been lost. Prior to 1871, Baldwin relied upon contract photographers, such as Coleman Sellers, to make photos of new locomotives. New York & Oswego Midland was a precursor to the New York, Ontario & Western. The locomotive, with three pairs of drivers, was among Baldwin's Class 8-28 D of the period. *Construction No. 2592, Railroad Museum of Pennsylvania (PHMC)*

Opposite: Baldwin built Central Railroad of New Jersey 4-4-0 No. 162 in May 1881. This image is a classic example of a wet-plate photograph, made just a few years before Baldwin switched to commercial dry-plate photography. It is unusual among Baldwin's builder photos from the period in that it was not opaqued and so reveals the buildings along the Philadelphia & Reading tracks near Baldwin's works in downtown Philadelphia. Visitors to the site today will find virtually nothing to indicate it was once the most productive locomotive works in the world. *Baldwin image No. 156, construction No. 5618, courtesy H. L. Broadbelt Baldwin Collection (RR88.2), Railroad Museum of Pennsylvania (PHMC)*

CHAPTER **ONE**

BALDWIN IN THE 19TH CENTURY

THE BALDWIN LOCOMOTIVE WORKS dates to the formative days of American railroading, and its early history was chronicled by the company over the years to become enshrined both in its lore and its advertising. By the mid-nineteenth century, the company was already boasting of its early achievements while celebrating the pioneering accomplishments of its founder, Matthias W. Baldwin. M. W. Baldwin died in 1866, but his company continued to grow into one of the best known names in locomotive building. (To distinguish the man from his enterprise, this text usually spells out the name of the individual or uses his initials along with his last name, while the Baldwin Locomotive Works is often referred to as simply "Baldwin.")

Much of what is known about the Baldwin Locomotive Works in its earliest years has emanated from the company's own archives and the work of pioneer railroad writers like Angus Sinclair, who set out to tell the story of American locomotives at the turn of the twentieth century. Aiding Baldwin's publicity efforts was the great public interest in railways during the formative era, resulting in contemporary accounts of early Baldwin locomotives. Patents by M. W. Baldwin and others also provide details on the locomotives. Crucial to understanding the relevance, significance, and technical details of Baldwin's earliest production are the writings of John H. White Jr., whose detailed research on nineteenth-century locomotive-building is among the

In the early 1830s, Camden & Amboy imported a Robert Stephenson–built locomotive. It was among the first locomotives inspected by young Matthias W. Baldwin before he began construction of his first full-size locomotive, known as *Old Ironsides*. Today, C&A's British import, known as the *John Bull*, is displayed at the Smithsonian in Washington, D.C. *Baldwin image No. 7933, courtesy H. L. Broadbelt Baldwin Collection (RR88.2), Railroad Museum of Pennsylvania (PHMC)*

most thorough and best presented railway literature available on the subject.

M. W. BALDWIN'S EARLY DAYS

Trained as jeweler, Matthias W. Baldwin was a Philadelphian who began his trade in 1817. A decline in demand for his jewelry-making skills led him to diversify his business, and in 1825 he formed a partnership with machinist David Mason to produce printing and book-binding tools. In the course of this business, M. W. Baldwin became involved in the production of stationary steam engines. The first of these was built to serve his company's own requirements, while later engines were built for commercial applications. Although M. W. Baldwin's partnership with Mason was dissolved by 1830, he continued with the production of industrial engines.

Practical steam locomotive technology first emerged in Britain in the early nineteenth century as an evolutionary outgrowth of the Industrial Revolution. By the mid-1820s, several significant British steam railway projects were underway, and the technology had caught the attention of industrialists in the United States. Among the earliest American railways were Pennsylvania schemes designed for the movement of coal. In 1829, Delaware & Hudson built a light tramway between Carbondale and Honesdale as part of its canal network, importing locomotives from Britain in a failed, formative attempt at steam railway propulsion. In tests, D&H found the locomotives too heavy for service. Other early American efforts resulted in more imports, as well as domestic attempts to build locomotives with varying degrees of success. Yet, while the potential of the steam locomotive gained acceptance, the foundation to produce this technology domestically for widespread application was still not ready in the early 1830s.

By that time, Philadelphia had emerged as one of America's foremost industrial centers, developing as an early transportation hub for primordial railroad schemes. This placed

M. W. Baldwin in an ideal position to design and build a railway locomotive, though his company made the jump from engine producer to locomotive builder in stages. In 1831 Franklin Peale of the Philadelphia Museum asked M. W. Baldwin to build a very small working locomotive engine as a display. In April, he delivered an engine based on drawings he had seen portraying the entrants in Britain's celebrated Rainhill Trials. M. W. Baldwin's miniature was sufficiently powerful to haul two small carriages with passengers on a loop in the museum grounds.

Peale further aided M. W. Baldwin's formative engine development by organizing the inspection of Camden & Amboy's recently imported British locomotive—known today as the *John Bull*. This significant early import was built by Robert Stephenson, son of early railroad builder George Stephenson. Robert's famed *Rocket* had won the Rainhill Trials and established the pattern for most subsequent steam locomotive design. *John Bull* was an early 0-4-0 type of the Samson type and considered among the most advanced machines of its day. White explains that a few months after he inspected *John Bull*, M. W. Baldwin supervised the assembly of another British import, named *Delaware*, bought by the Newcastle & Frenchtown Railroad in Delaware. This locomotive also set M. W. Baldwin's mind to work.

In 1832, M. W. Baldwin's locomotive expertise with British engines and his established reputation as a skilled machinist led to his first full-sized locomotive commission by the recently opened Philadelphia, Germantown & Norristown Railroad. To fulfill this order, M. W. Baldwin's company built a near copy of Robert Stephenson's successful Planet type that used the 2-2-0 wheel arrangement (like Stephenson's *Delaware*). Baldwin's pioneering American-built locomotive, known as *Old Ironsides*, was tested on November 23, 1832. It featured 54-inch driving wheels, 45-inch leading wheels, 9½x18–inch cylinders, and a 30-inch-diameter boiler. Difficulties with this first machine led to operating frustrations.

From an early date, American railroads were built to different standards than their British counterparts. British lines tended to be well-capitalized, highly engineered, and built with solid tracks on a near level with gentle curves. American lines, which tended

to be underfunded, were built to a lighter standard, which often resulted in more undulating profiles, sharper curves, and more flexible track bed. British-style locomotives engineered for high track standards featured a rigid suspension, were poorly suited for American track, and so had a tendency to derail. Early on, locomotive designers recognized a need for locomotive types that would better hold to American-style track. Ultimately, locomotives designed for American track required a flexible wheelbase and guide wheels to operate successfully. (Camden & Amboy's Isaac Dripps fitted a guiding pilot-truck to the imported *John Bull*.) M. W. Baldwin recognizing the flaws in his domestically built Planet type and engineered changes on his company's second locomotive.

BALDWIN 4-2-0

In 1833–1834, Baldwin built a locomotive for the South Carolina Railroad on the request of E. H. Miller, a prominent Charlestonian acting as an agent for the line. On Miller's suggestion, M. W. Baldwin adopted a leading truck devised by John B. Jervis in 1832. This greatly improved the locomotive's

Matthias W. Baldwin's first full-sized locomotive was patterned after the recently developed Planet type in Britain. Completed in 1832 for the Philadelphia, Germantown & Norristown Railroad, it weighed about five tons and was sold for about $4,000. The original was scrapped many years ago, and this model was often used by the Baldwin Locomotive Works to represent its historic pioneer. *Courtesy H. L. Broadbelt Baldwin Collection (RR88.2), Railroad Museum of Pennsylvania (PHMC)*

SPECIFICATIONS
Philadelphia & Reading *Neversink*
Wheel arrangement: 4-2-0
Cylinders: Two 10½x16 in.
Drivers: 54 in.
Total engine weight: 22,950 lbs.
Tractive effort: n/a

Ordered by Philadelphia & Reading in 1836 and delivered in 1837, *Neversink* was the fortieth locomotive built by Baldwin. It was typical of the 4-2-0 types built by Baldwin and other early locomotive builders in the mid-1830s. *Railroad Museum of Pennsylvania (PHMC)*

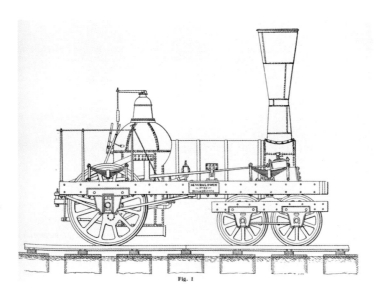

Fig. 1

tracking ability and overcame rigidity associated with British locomotive design. Baldwin No. 2, named *E. H. Miller*, was delivered in 1834. Its 4-2-0 wheel arrangement, although not unique to Baldwin, was soon adopted as the company's standard. In his 1907 book, *Development of the Locomotive Engine*, Angus Sinclair explains that this locomotive's 4-2-0 arrangement essentially established the parameters for what developed as the first national locomotive type: Soon, the 4-2-0 evolved into the 4-4-0 American type, which predominated in mid-nineteenth-century America.

Key to Baldwin's successful 4-2-0 design were a horizontal boiler, a single pair of drivers, and the Jervis-designed leading truck positioned under the smokebox. Locomotives at this time used inside cylinders (enclosed inside the smokebox) and were inside-connected (referring to the location of the drive rods that link the piston rods with drive wheels and thus transmit power from pistons to wheels). Among Baldwin's refinements was M. W. Baldwin's patented half-crank axle, which offered simplified axle construction that connected the crank portions of the axle directly to the driving wheels.

Baldwin further refined the 4-2-0 with its third locomotive. This machine was ordered by the Philadelphia & Trenton

but ultimately was delivered to Pennsylvania's "state road," the Philadelphia & Columbia—a line operated at the eastern end of the famed Main Line of Public Works (the state-owned system of canals and railroads). Known as the *Lancaster* after the Pennsylvania city along the line, this locomotive was profiled by White in his book *American Locomotives: An Engineering History 1830–1880*. Baldwin charged the P&C $5,580 for the *Lancaster*, and the engine entered service on June 28, 1834. It featured 9x16-inch cylinders and 54-inch drivers, weighed 15,000 pounds, and worked at 120 pounds operating pressure—considered relatively high pressure at the time. Initially, the *Lancaster* was used in construction of the railroad's second main track. White notes that the locomotive performed well in service. It was rated to haul 35 tons but in one instance was noted for moving a 16-car train weighing 75 tons. (At that time, the "long ton," 2,240 pounds, was still the American standard.) This may seem like a tiny amount for a locomotive to haul when single loaded freight cars today routinely weight more than 100 tons (2,000-pound measure) and freight trains may weigh as much as 20,000 tons, but in 1834, when railroading was in its infancy, weights and train sizes were judged on a much smaller scale.

Once Baldwin had settled on the 4-2-0 wheel arrangement—designated its Class B type—the company clung to this simple design for a number of years and refrained from adopting more advanced types put forth by competitors. Baldwin continued to advance the soon obsolete 4-2-0 for years after other builders were forwarding the 4-4-0 arrangement, developed in 1836, which became the most universally adopted locomotive type of the nineteenth century.

White notes that Baldwin built more than 100 4-2-0s between 1834 and 1842. During this time, the company implemented a variety of improvements to the design, including the change from outside-frame construction to inside frames, which would become standard practice in American locomotive design. Baldwin's last outside-frame 4-2-0 was built in 1839. Even after the company designed and adapted newer types, the 4-2-0 remained the standard type in its locomotive catalog, with two B types offered in 1855, more than 20 years after the type was introduced.

LOCOMOTIVE MANUFACTURING SUCCESS

Baldwin's early success as a locomotive manufacturer led the company to construct new erecting shops on Broad Street in Philadelphia in 1835, not far from today's Center City. Gradually, as the company's business grew and flourished, it expanded these facilities, and by the early twentieth century it covered eight square blocks.

From 1835 onward, Baldwin focused its business on the locomotive trade that for many years accounted for nearly all of the company's orders. Baldwin's 1881 *Illustrated Catalog* noted the company had completed its 11th locomotive by May 1835, and the *History of the Baldwin Locomotive Works 1831–1923*

(authored anonymously by Baldwin's Paul T. Warner) highlights significant production statistics and milestones that mark Baldwin's success as a locomotive manufacturer. Baldwin completed 5 locomotives in 1834, 14 in 1835, and 40 in 1836. The cyclical nature of the locomotive business was a reflection on the growth of the railroads and the cyclical boom-and-bust nature of nineteenth-century business. Where the early 1840s saw a significant drop in locomotive orders, annual production by the middle of the decade exceeded 40 units per year, only to be reduced by half over the next few years. In 1851, Baldwin built 50 locomotives, its highest number to date, reflecting the effective capacity of its works at that time. Continued expansion of the company's

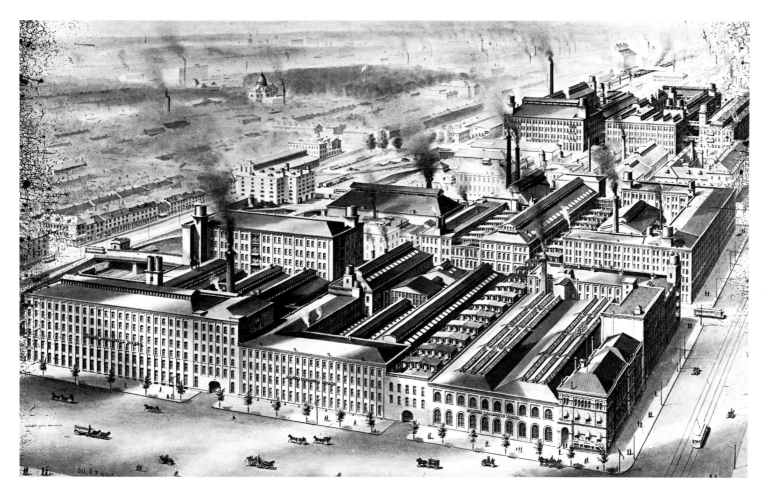

This period artist's vision depicts the Baldwin Locomotive Works' downtown Philadelphia plant at Broad and Spring Garden streets. At its peak in the early twentieth century, this plant covered eight city blocks, employed more than 17,000 people, and could turn out as many as 2,600 locomotives annually. In 1906, Baldwin began phasing the downtown plant out in favor of its new Eddystone facility. A hundred years later, there is virtually no visible trace of this once expansive facility. *Courtesy H. L. Broadbelt Baldwin Collection (RR88.2), Railroad Museum of Pennsylvania (PHMC)*

factory allowed for greater production numbers so that by 1864, it crested the 100-locomotive mark for the first time, producing 130 engines in one year.

While its production totals continued to ebb and flow depending on demand and Baldwin's marketing and design skills, its annual production total would not drop below the 100 mark until the Great Depression in the 1930s. By 1880, the company was building more than 500 engines annually, and in 1890 it crested the 900-engine mark. Baldwin built its 1,000th locomotive in 1861, its 2,000th locomotive in 1869, and its 5,000th locomotive in 1880. By the turn of the twentieth century, Baldwin had built nearly 18,000 steam locomotives and was by far the most productive locomotive manufacturer in North America.

AMERICAN STANDARD

The 4-4-0 was patented and first built in 1836 by Philadelphia, Germantown & Norristown's engineer Henry Campbell, a close acquaintance of M. W. Baldwin and a fellow Philadelphian. The type was significantly improved upon in 1838 by Eastwick & Harrison's development of an equalization lever that gave the locomotive a three-point suspension for better tracking ability and greater pulling power. Baldwin continued to build 4-2-0s in

Built in March 1880, Baldwin's 5,000th locomotive was designed for fast passenger service on the Philadelphia & Reading. It was a rare example of a Baldwin Class A type, which by definition used a single set of drivers for high-speed passenger operations. A letter in Baldwin's files dated May 14, 1880, from P&R's J. E. Wootten states it made an express run of 89.4 miles in 98 minutes. When P&R ran into financial difficulties, Baldwin took the locomotive back and resold it to Lovett Eames, inventor of a vacuum brake system, who sent it to England for demonstration purposes. A period press release explained the engine was sold for scrap in 1884. Although not adopted on a wide scale in the United States, vacuum braking systems were a standard for many years in Great Britain. *Baldwin image No. 145, construction No. 5000, courtesy H. L. Broadbelt Baldwin Collection (RR88.2), Railroad Museum of Pennsylvania (PHMC)*

significant quantities until 1845, when the company finally acquiesced to the success of the 4-4-0. Once the 4-4-0 was adopted, Baldwin became a fervent supporter, building many thousands of the type over the next 80 years.

The 4-4-0's well-balanced design, flexible three-point suspension with excellent tractive effort, and high degree of adaptability contributed to its popularity on American railroads and its popular "American" designation. A 4-4-0 offered greater tractive effort than a 4-2-0 without significantly increasing locomotive weight or axle load. Depending on the diameter of the driving wheels, 4-4-0s could work in either freight or passenger service, with many designed to accommodate both kinds of work with relative ease.

Baldwin designated the type as its Class C, indicating that it had two pairs of driving wheels. Warner explains that Baldwin's first 4-4-0 was built in 1845 for the South Carolina Railroad, with Baldwin buying patent rights from Campbell and the rights to the equalization beams from Eastwick & Harrison. This cab-less engine with a Bury (hemispherical) firebox was typical of Baldwin engines from the period. It featured 13¾x18-inch cylinders and 60-inch driving wheels, and weighed approximately 30,000 pounds (specifications indicate 15 tons). Although it used outside cylinders, it was inside-connected, using Baldwin's half-crank axle.

Over the years, as the demands of railroads required more powerful locomotives, the proportions of Baldwin's 4-4-0s were scaled upward; the locomotives of this basic arrangement built later in the century were substantially larger and heavier than the early machines, and far more capable.

Baldwin's Class 8-28 C, an anthracite-burner built about 1880 for the Camden & Atlantic, was featured prominently in Baldwin's 1881 *Illustrated Catalog* with 17x22-inch cylinders and 66-inch driving wheels, and weighing 77,000 pounds in working order with 52,000 pounds on driving wheels. A letter from C&A's master mechanic, Rufus Hill, reprinted in the *Illustrated Catalog* highlights this locomotive's performance: Hauling a train consisting of six cars (four passenger cars, one parlor car, and a baggage car) weighing 323,725 pounds including the

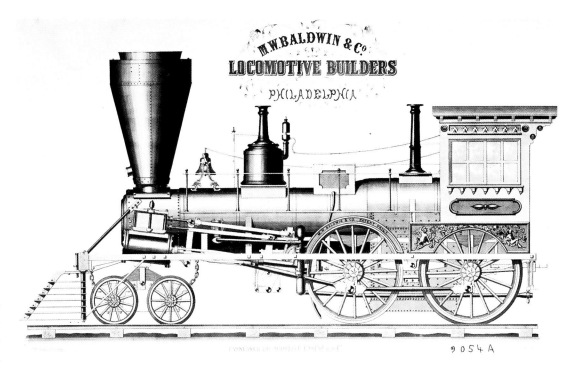

passengers and baggage, the locomotive and tender (with 3,000 gallons of water) weighed 133,000 pounds, for a total weight of 456,725 pounds. The train departed Camden, New Jersey, at 4:32 p.m. and arrived at Atlantic City at 5:47 p.m., taking 75 minutes to travel 58.59 miles. This included a short section of 4-mile-per-hour operation near Atlantic City where there was a slow-order across a drawbridge. At times, the engine clipped along at nearly a mile a minute, a pretty impressive performance for the early 1880s.

FLEXIBLE-BEAM-TRUCK ENGINES

By the 1840s, railroad freight business had become the fastest growing and most significant portion of total traffic, and some railroads, like Pennsylvania anthracite haulers, derived very large revenue from freight haulage. To satisfy the demand for more effective freight haulers, locomotive builders were faced with the task of providing more powerful locomotives capable of negotiating a railroad's lightly built track and tight curvature.

Although the company resisted production of the 4-4-0 wheel arrangement until 1845, after that time it embraced the type enthusiastically and included several plans for 4-4-0s in its catalog. This image depicts a typical Baldwin Class C passenger-service 4-4-0 from 1854. It features independent, variable cutoff and driving wheels 72 inches in diameter. Prior to the advent of practical commercial photography, Baldwin relied on artist-rendered illustrations to portray its locomotives. *Baldwin image No. 09054, courtesy H. L. Broadbelt Baldwin Collection (RR88.2), Railroad Museum of Pennsylvania (PHMC)*

PAUL T. WARNER: BALDWIN'S SILENT HISTORIAN

Born in Philadelphia on September 7, 1877, to Massah and Celestine Reink Warner, Paul Theodore Warner grew up in West Philadelphia in the 1880s and 1890s, where he watched the Pennsylvania Railroad. Observing the Pennsy's 4-4-0s in action led him to become a lifelong student of the locomotive and a pioneering engine enthusiast long before organized railfan activity took root. Like many men of his era, he became acquainted with locomotives by riding on them as well as watching them pass. He also actively photographed locomotives at the turn of the century and is considered among the earliest noncommercial photographers in the East to make action photographs. His images date to 1897 when he photographed Lackawanna and Pennsy trains. In a 1997 interview with railroad historian Kurt Bell, George M. Hart related the details of his friend Warner's first cab ride:

> [This] was on a Reading "bicycle" type 4-2-2. This was 1901 and the engine was the 317. It had been renumbered about a year before from 378, I believe. This was the New York Express, which was an hourly express that carried three cars. It was a Camelback, and he must have ridden in the cab—not on the fireman's side, but on the engineer's side. He told me that they had a very hard job of getting the train out on schedule, or keeping on schedule, between the Reading Terminal and Fern Rock Grade. When they got to the Fern Rock Grade, the engineer said to him, "First, we got no steam. Now, we got steam, but we got no sand."

Warner worked for a number of years as an electrical engineer at Baldwin, and in 1917–1918 served as the company's assistant advertising manager. Later, he earned the job of Baldwin Locomotive Works librarian and historian. Among his duties was editing *Baldwin Locomotives* magazine, for which he researched and wrote many detailed articles on the company's locomotives. During his many years at Baldwin he was in close contact with the photographic collection that composes much of this book. During the 1930s, Warner shared a partner's desk at Baldwin with locomotive designer Eddie O. Elliott, who had designed earlier locomotives for the Philadelphia & Reading. The two men would converse for hours on locomotive design and history. Hart recalled, "When I was down at Baldwin's, there would be two desks . . . big desks. Paul Warner sat at the one desk and Eddie Elliot was at the other. And they would face each other. . . . There wasn't much left to be known about the parts of a steam locomotive between those two men."

Paul shared his enthusiasm with many of the pioneer locomotive historians. He often went through the Baldwin files, sorting out duplicate material like old catalogs, magazines, Records of Recent Construction, and photo specification cards and distributing them to his friends Thomas Taber and Walter Lucas, themselves pioneering railway enthusiasts of the era. His personal correspondence with others reveals his deep affection for the subject and concern for the details and particulars of the engines, and he often spent considerable time finding answers to all queries. His talks at Philadelphia's Franklin Institute and his 10 articles in the Railway & Locomotive Historical Society Bulletin inspired a number of the leading railway historians of his era. Although rarely seen, his own photographs were extraordinary, and he used his talent to capture more than just passing locomotives but the changing landscape around him, oceangoing ships, and friends and family.

Warner's work contributed greatly to the body of literature drawn upon in the research and writing of this text. Although often a silent author, his hand can be found in a great variety of documents and texts originating from Baldwin during his years there. Frederick Westing, who worked with Warner at Baldwin, attributes the *History of the Baldwin Locomotive Works 1831–1923* to Warner's pen. In his own version of this text, *The Locomotives That Baldwin Built*, Westing writes that Warner was "the greatest American locomotive historian" and credits him with "phenomenal" knowledge of the company's engines.

In 1948 Warner suffered a heart attack that resulted in his permanent retirement in 1952. This event was marked by correspondence with George Hart:

> *I have now been on the "retired list" since November 28 [1952], and am gradually getting used to the new situation. They really gave me a grand send-off at Eddystone. I had interviews with the President and several of the V.P.'s, and spent most of the day calling on my friends. I'll get a pension—not a large one, but it will at least buy my clothes—and the boys took up a collection and they gave given me a Philco Radio-phonograph which was most unexpected. Things were said which almost started the tears running down my cheeks, so you may imagine that I felt pretty good when I left.*

Paul T. Warner, longtime Baldwin librarian and historian, assembled detailed photo albums featuring the company's engines. After his death these passed to his friend George T. Hart, who, in turn, willed them to the Railroad Museum of Pennsylvania. This rare image portrays a group of new Baldwin 4-4-0s polished and ready to leave for the 1893 Columbian Exposition in Chicago. *John S. Powell photo, Warner album, courtesy George M. Hart Collection (RR2005.39), Railroad Museum of Pennsylvania (PHMC)*

Warner continued to study locomotives in his retirement, traveling extensively throughout the United States and Canada, and died at Moravian Manor in Easton, Pennsylvania, on February 11, 1967, at the age of 89. He was buried in Nisky Hill Cemetery in Easton. His collection of papers went by bequest to his friends Walter A. Lucas and George M. Hart. When Lucas died on August 19, 1967, Warner's entire collection landed in Hart's custody and remained inaccessible until its donation to the Railroad Museum of Pennsylvania in October 2008.

Special thanks to Kurt Bell, archivist at the Railroad Museum of Pennsylvania, and John Gruber of the Center for Railroad Photography and Art for help with this sidebar.

Baldwin's negative files include a copy photo of Pennsylvania Railroad No. 216, built by Baldwin in August 1861. This was one of Baldwin's six-wheel, flexible-beam-truck engines. While the flexible-beam-truck engines represented a significant portion of Baldwin's production from the mid-1840s until the 1860s, images of these locomotives at the plant are rare because commercial photography was in its infancy. *Baldwin image No. 8343, courtesy H. L. Broadbelt Baldwin Collection (RR88.2), Railroad Museum of Pennsylvania (PHMC)*

Baldwin's solution was the novel flexible-beam-truck locomotive for which M. W. Baldwin received U.S. Patent No. 2,759 on August 25, 1842. This unusual locomotive type delivered great tractive effort by placing its full adhesive weight on drivers while featuring a sufficiently flexible wheelbase to negotiate track conditions. Key to the design was M. W. Baldwin's flexible-beam truck, which, as Baldwin explained in his patent, "to the turning or running upon curved portions of a railroad more perfectly adapt themselves to any vertical inequities of the rails." The truck held the pair of forward axles; thus, these four wheels acted both as drivers and as guides (in a manner similar to locomotives equipped with leading bogies).

Unlike a bogie truck, such as the leading truck designed by John Jervis in 1832, the leading flexible-beam truck enabled the driving axles to slide back and forth laterally while remaining parallel to each other and the axle located on the rigid wheelbase. It was crucial to ensure the powered axles remained parallel to each other to avoid difficulties with the connecting rods that powered the drive wheels. White notes that it was only necessary to allow for slight parallel movement of the front axles in order to give a locomotive necessary lateral flexibility. By paying close attention to design details, Baldwin was able to build locomotives of this type that were remarkably successful during the 1840s and 1850s.

Initially, Baldwin built flexible-beam engines with an 0-6-0 wheel arrangement (three powered axles). Cylinders were set on an incline and powered the rear rigid-mounted drivers. The first of the type was completed at the end of 1842 for the Philadelphia & Reading. According to Warner, this 18-ton engine was capable of moving up to 150 loaded cars weighing a total of 1,130 tons downgrade from Schuylkill Haven to Philadelphia at a top speed of 7 miles per hour. A variation of the type used a 2-4-0 arrangement.

Although M. W. Baldwin's 1842 patent made provisions for an eight-coupled, flexible-beam engine, it wasn't until 1846 that Baldwin expanded the concept to an 0-8-0. The first of these was an engine named *Atlas* for the Philadelphia & Reading. White estimates that the 0-8-0 variation accounted for approximately 150 locomotives built over the next 20 years and calculates that, in total, about 310 flexible-beam-truck engines were constructed between their introduction and the end of production in 1866. By then, the type was functionally obsolete because it was only useful for very slow-speed freight services. As railroads improved their physical plant and built heavier track, they ordered more conventionally designed locomotives capable of higher tractive effort and greater speeds than the old flexible-beam-truck engines.

DESIGN CHANGES

The earliest American locomotives were relatively small and minimalist machines, functional in appearance and equipped with neither cabs nor whistles. During the 1840s, the American-designed locomotives took on the form and accoutrements for which they would become best known.

Baldwin's first locomotives with crew protection were 0-8-0 flexible-beam engines built for the P&R in 1846 and fitted with simple roofs. This rudimentary protection soon evolved into a locomotive cab. In addition, simple and Spartan treatments on the earliest locomotives soon gave way to more colorful machines as railroads, railroaders, and finally builders began decorating locomotives in brighter colors and polished metal, while adding embellishments and flourishes, including brass fittings, tuned brass bells, and multi-chime whistles.

A variety of technological changes evolved as well during this crucial stage of development. Early Baldwin engines had featured the hemispherical Bury firebox favored by the early British imports. Later locomotive design embraced the wagon-top boiler, which was standard by 1850. Other improvements in basic technology included more advanced types of valves and valve gear (the equipment used to regulate the admission of steam into the cylinders). In 1861, steel was introduced into locomotive construction. Warner notes that steel was first used in fireboxes for an order of Pennsylvania Railroad locomotives. After the American Civil War, Baldwin made steel firebox construction standard. By 1868, steel boiler tubes and steel boilers had been adopted as well.

NEW TYPES AND BIGGER ENGINES

Angus Sinclair credits Baldwin's Philadelphia-based competitor, Norris, with building the first 4-6-0 Ten-Wheeler in 1847. This was the logical expansion of existing types, blending the

This copy photo from the Baldwin collection portrays Pennsylvania Railroad No. 1014, an 1861-built freight-service 4-6-0. The 4-6-0 Ten-Wheeler emerged as a popular heavy freight locomotive in the middle years of the nineteenth century, and the type continued to evolve over the next 50 years. By the late nineteenth century, the type was more commonly used for passenger services than for freight. *Baldwin image No. 8349, courtesy H. L. Broadbelt Baldwin Collection (RR88.2), Railroad Museum of Pennsylvania (PHMC)*

224 M. W. Baldwin & Co., (Order No. 1015) Built to a ... few slight changes made at Altoona Shops in 1862. Originally the wheel covers extended downward between the drivers and sandboxes were under them between first and second pairs of drivers. Injectorcheckvalves were on side sheets of firebox. Straight stack was used. Otherwise photo shows engine as built.

SPECIFICATIONS

North Pennsylvania

Wyoming

Wheel arrangement: 4-6-0

Cylinders: Two 19x22 in.

Drivers: 50 in.

Total engine weight: estimated 54,000 lbs.

Tractive effort: 14,400 lbs.

This is a very rare photograph, collected by Paul T. Warner, depicting North Pennsylvania Railroad's 4-6-0 *Wyoming*. When it was built in May 1860, it was among the heaviest locomotives to emerge from the Baldwin Locomotive Works. Notice the inclined cylinders and the feed-water pump attached to the drive rods beneath the cab. Opened in 1855, in its heyday North Pennsylvania was the third largest railroad serving Philadelphia. Its main line extended northward to Bethlehem and had unfulfilled ambitions of reaching Buffalo. North Penn was merged into Philadelphia & Reading in 1879. *Construction No. 923, Warner album, courtesy George M. Hart Collection (RR2005.39), Railroad Museum of Pennsylvania (PHMC)*

advantages of a four-wheel guiding truck with a six-coupled engine. In 1852, Baldwin constructed its first Ten-Wheelers to fulfill a Pennsylvania Railroad order for heavy bituminous-burning, mountain-climbing engines. Gradually, the 4-6-0 was established as a standard type, first for freight, then for passenger work. Freight-service of the 4-6-0 superseded that of Baldwin's flexible-beam engines in the 1860s, and the type ultimately became one of the most popular wheel arrangements for general service during the late nineteenth century.

In the mid-1860s, the 2-6-0 Mogul type was developed. This had three pairs of drivers led by a Bissel pony truck. The first 2-6-0s with a leading pony truck were built by Baldwin's competitor, Rogers, around 1863. Baldwin adopted the type in 1867 and built its first engine, *E. A. Douglas*, for the Thomas Iron Company. The guiding wheels eased the locomotive through curves while allowing for the majority of the engine weight to be placed on drivers for better adhesion. Most early Moguls were constructed for heavy freight service.

CONSOLIDATIONS

The leading Bissel pony truck soon facilitated development of another, even more significant, wheel arrangement. In 1866, Alexander Mitchell, a young and dynamic master mechanic of the Lehigh & Mahanoy Railroad, submitted a plan to the Baldwin Locomotive Works for a very powerful freight-hauling locomotive designed for the steeply graded Mahanoy Plane. Employing four pairs of drivers, Mitchell proposed the first application of the 2-8-0 arrangement, intending not just a powerful freight engine but one that could maintain faster speeds while causing less damage to tracks than types already in service. White

In 1835, George Burnham began working with Matthias W. Baldwin in the construction of engines. After the latter's death in 1866, Burnham was made a company partner. His detailed knowledge and understanding of locomotives was typical of the men who ran the company in the nineteenth century. These pages are an entry from Burnham's personal notebook. Pictured is a Baldwin Class 7-B-1, a specialized variety of 4-2-0T built for the Rock River Railroad in 1868. *Railroad Museum of Pennsylvania (PHMC)*

George Burnham's notebook entry from 1866 records the details of the first 2-8-0 Consolidation, arguably the most influential locomotive built by Baldwin in the 1860s. Although frequently credited as being built for the Lehigh Valley, this locomotive was ordered by Alexander Mitchell of the Lehigh & Mahanoy Railroad, a line soon consolidated with the Lehigh Valley (hence "Consolidation"). All the relevant technical particulars of this pioneer machine are recorded on the right-hand page in Burnham's script. *Railroad Museum of Pennsylvania (PHMC)*

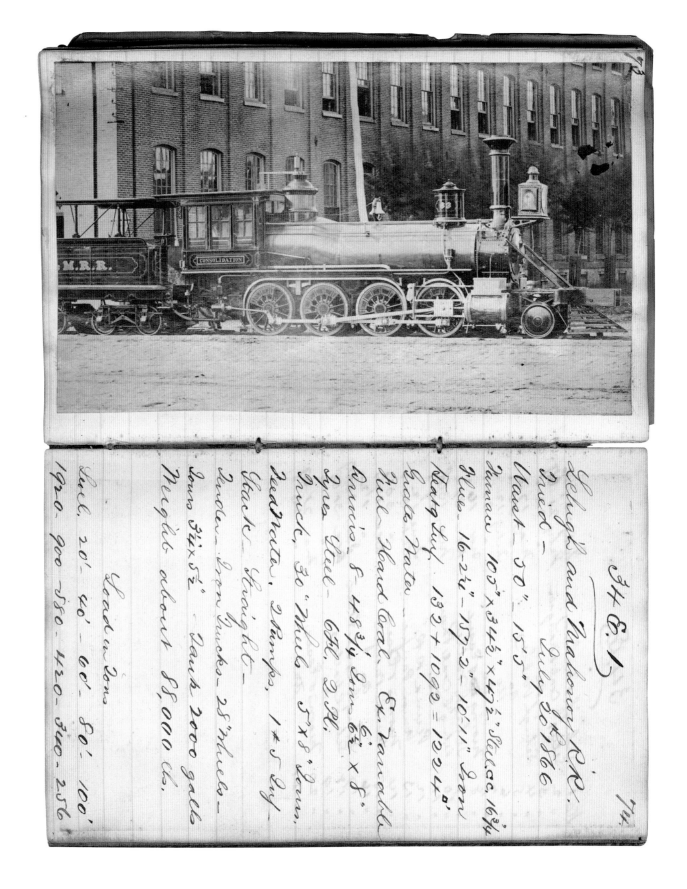

notes that Mitchell was working with Baldwin's Matthew Baird, who initially rejected his 2-8-0 proposal and instead encouraged Mitchell to buy one of Baldwin's flexible-beam-truck engines. From Baird's perspective, the flexible-beam engines offered a well-tested design proven to be well suited to graded operations. Yet, Mitchell was not impressed. The flexible-beam engines, while powerful, were also ponderously slow. He wanted a faster engine and finally convinced Baird to have Baldwin build the 2-8-0. This groundbreaking locomotive was appropriately named the Consolidation type to commemorate the merger of Mitchell's Lehigh & Mahanoy with the Lehigh Valley.

Based on its immediate success, the 2-8-0 type soon developed into the most successful freight locomotive in North America and was exported around the world. White writes that Mitchell "probably had little idea that he had created what was to become the most popular and widely built freight locomotive in the United States."

The combination of leading truck and high adhesion gave the 2-8-0 flexibility, power, and speed, which made it very desirable as a moderate-speed freight hauler. The 2-8-0 made most older types of eight-coupled locomotives functionally obsolete. With the coming of the 2-6-0 and 2-8-0, there was no longer any advantage to engines like Baldwin's flexible-beam-truck locomotives or ponderous curiosities like Ross Winans' 0-8-0 "Camels" (not to be confused with the "camelback" arrangement exhibited on some 2-8-0s).

Scranton, Pennsylvania–based anthracite-hauler Delaware, Lackawanna & Western was an early user of Consolidations. In 1876, Baldwin built five heavy 2-8-0s for its mainline freight service. Last of the lot was No. 130 *Goliath*. After 25 years of hard service it was scrapped in favor of much larger Consolidations. In its day, a locomotive like this commanded $11,450—a lot of money back when common laborers earned only a dollar a day. *Baldwin image No. 63, construction No. 3911, courtesy H. L. Broadbelt Baldwin Collection (RR88.2), Railroad Museum of Pennsylvania (PHMC)*

SPECIFICATIONS

New York, West Shore & Buffalo No. 128

Wheel arrangement: 2-8-0

Cylinders: Two 20x24 in.

Drivers: 50 in.

Total engine weight: 113,000 lbs.

Tractive effort: n/a

New York, West Shore & Buffalo 2-8-0 No. 128 was built as part of an order for 30 similar locomotives during 1883 and 1884. These featured straight-top boilers instead of the more common wagon-top boiler. Pennsylvania Railroad interests built NYWS&B along the west shore of the Hudson River to Albany then west to Buffalo to compete with the parallel New York Central & Hudson River Railroad's famed Water Level Route. Soon after it opened, the line entered the New York Central & Hudson River family as part of a complex deal with the Pennsy negotiated by J. P. Morgan. *Baldwin image No. 210, construction No. 7049, courtesy H. L. Broadbelt Baldwin Collection (RR88.2), Railroad Museum of Pennsylvania (PHMC)*

As with most wheel arrangements, the 2-8-0 was not exclusive to Baldwin but was constructed by virtually every large commercial North American locomotive manufacturer. It remained the standard road-freight locomotive on most lines until the advent of the 2-8-2 Mikado type, and even then some railroads continued to prefer 2-8-0s. In his book *The Steam Locomotive in America*, Alfred Bruce explains that "the [2-8-0] was built in the United States in greater numbers than any other

Built in 1886, Lehigh & Hudson River Railway 2-6-0 No. 9, *John Rutherford*, was a camelback type with a Wootten firebox for burning anthracite and an awning designed to shelter the fireman. In the place of a traditional sand dome, this engine featured a more unusual sandbox above the leading drive wheels. *Baldwin image No. 284, construction No. 7979, courtesy H. L. Broadbelt Baldwin Collection (RR88.2), Railroad Museum of Pennsylvania (PHMC)*

wheel arrangement—over 33,000, of which about 21,000 were in U.S. main-line service."

Over the years, the 2-8-0 was adapted in a variety of ways, using different types of boilers and fireboxes, as well as improved varieties of valves and valve gear. The anthracite railroads ordered 2-8-0s with wide fireboxes, and many of these were built as "camelbacks." The great width of the firebox precluded conventional placement of the engineer's cab and resulted in a

Fitchburg Railroad 2-8-0 No. 90 was built as part of an order for six Consolidations in 1881. No. 90 used 20x24-inch cylinders and drivers slightly larger than 50 inches. Instead of the more common wagon-top boiler, this locomotive featured a straight-top boiler favored by New England railroads of the period. Fitchburg was integrated into the Boston & Maine network in 1900. Later, this locomotive was converted for use as an 0-8-0 switcher. *Baldwin image No. 103, construction No. 5512, courtesy H. L. Broadbelt Baldwin Collection (RR88.2), Railroad Museum of Pennsylvania (PHMC)*

SPECIFICATIONS
Philadelphia & Reading No. 415
Wheel arrangement: 2-8-0
Cylinders: Two 20x24 in.
Grate Area: 76 sq.ft.
Drivers: 50 in.
Total engine weight: 104,100 lbs.
Tractive effort: n/a

In the 1870s, Philadelphia & Reading's general manager, John E. Wootten, patented a boiler designed to burn anthracite fines (very small pieces). The boiler required a broad, shallow firebox with a large grate. P&R built the first locomotive with the Wootten firebox in 1878. The great width of the firebox precluded conventional placement of the engineer's cab and resulted in a split-position design that separated work areas for the engineer and fireman in an arrangement commonly described as a "camelback." This Baldwin-built camelback Consolidation dates from 1880 and was typical of the very early applications of Wootten's patent. *Baldwin image No. 38, construction No. 4935, courtesy H. L. Broadbelt Baldwin Collection (RR88.2), Railroad Museum of Pennsylvania (PHMC)*

split-position design that separated the engineer's and fireman's work areas. The unusual placement of the cab astride the boiler resulted in the descriptive camelback name. Also, the 2-8-0 was adapted by many builders with various arrangements of compound cylinders. Later, in the early years of the twentieth century, when superheating became popular (see Chapters 2 and 3), many railroads rebuilt existing 2-8-0s for superheated operation, and many new 2-8-0s were ordered so equipped.

Not many years after the first 2-8-0 was built for the Lehigh Valley, the type was adapted to narrow gauge service, and in the last decades of the nineteenth century, the 2-8-0 became one of the most common types of narrow gauge locomotive built by Baldwin for domestic freight applications.

Reprinted in Baldwin's 1881 *Illustrated Catalogue of Locomotives* were letters from various railroad officials describing the details of Baldwin Consolidations in service. Perhaps most interesting among these is one from none other than Alexander Mitchell, then of Lehigh Valley Railroad's Wyoming Division, dated December 12, 1871, that describes the Class 10-34 E, the lighter of the two Baldwin catalog-standard 2-8-0s:

Messrs. M. Baird & Co.:

Gentlemen, We have now in service 10 locomotives of the Consolidation class, constructed at your works. The first engine of this pattern was put in

According to Baldwin records, this three-foot-gauge 2-8-0 was built in 1873 for Pennsylvania's East Broad Top as its No. 3. However, the locomotive was instead sold to Denver & Rio Grande, becoming its No. 13, *Mosca.* Since it was narrow gauge, it was proportionally smaller than a standard gauge Consolidation. *Baldwin image No. 5, construction No. 3475, courtesy H. L. Broadbelt Baldwin Collection (RR88.2), Railroad Museum of Pennsylvania (PHMC)*

use on the Mahanoy grade in 1866, and the others have been added from time to time for working this and other inclines. Our experience with this style of engine has been thorough and extended, and we are satisfied as to their qualifications for working heavy grades and hauling maximum loads.

The result of our experience with these machines may be stated as follows:

Steaming. Anthracite coal is used as fuel, and steam is generated freely and abundantly.

Speed. These engines are run with their trains at speeds from 10 to 20 miles per hour, and we have occasionally hauled passenger trains with them, particularly in winter, when they are of special service in clearing the track of snow.

Traversing Curves. These engines are run on parts of the line having curves of 410' radius, and they pass these curves without difficulty, and will also enter short curves in switches, and pass around any of our curves as readily as do our 8- or 10-wheeled engines.

Wear of Track. We have no evidence that they wear the track more in hauling trains than other engines.

Loads Hauled. We have on this division one long grade of 1' in 55', or 96' per mile, for 12 miles in length, with curves of 573' radius, several of the them being reverse, and short tangents. The regular load of these engines on this grade is 33 loaded cars, equal to 280 gross tons.

Descending Grades. We use no appliance for retarding the engine in descending grades except the tender brake. With brakes on all eight of the tender wheels one of these engines is held without difficulty on the grade named.

Consumption of Fuel and Stores. The quantity of fuel and stores used by these engines is less in proportion to load and mileage than that of the

other engines we have in service. As a practical evidence of the estimation in which this class of power is held by our company, I may refer to the order recently placed with you for 5 more of these engines for delivery in February and March.

Yours truly,
A. Mitchell,
Division Superintendent

DECAPODS

In 1867, soon after the delivery of the first 2-8-0, Alexander Mitchell ordered a pair of 2-10-0 "Decapods" from Baldwin's competitor, Norris. Baldwin first built this type for export to Mexico in 1881 and Brazil in 1885. An article by Paul T. Warner in the April 1925 *Baldwin Locomotives* explains that Baldwin's Brazilian Decapods stirred renewed interest in the type domestically. A similar type of 2-10-0 was ordered by Northern Pacific in 1886, and in 1891, Erie Railroad (then known as the New York, Lake Erie & Western) bought some exceptionally large 2-10-0s in the camelback configuration for use as helpers over Gulf Summit in Pennsylvania. These weighed 195,000 pounds.

Although the Decapod would never achieve the widespread popularity enjoyed by the 2-8-0, the wheel arrangement was further developed in the twentieth century. Santa Fe, which had ordered the type for helper service on Raton Pass at the Colorado–New Mexico border, was the first to make the next adaptation of the 10-coupled type, in 1902 expanding it into the 2-10-2, which became known as the Santa Fe type (see Chapters 2 and 3).

DIVERSIFICATION

After the American Civil War and Matthias W. Baldwin's death in 1866, Baldwin made serious efforts to diversify its locomotive business and expand its market. Among these efforts was increasing business in the export market. This aspect of locomotive production was not new to the company—it had exported

Ten years after the company had reluctantly constructed the first of the type for Alexander Mitchell, Baldwin built this Lehigh Valley Consolidation. By 1876, the 2-8-0 had proven its abilities as a heavy freight hauler and was on its way to becoming the most common locomotive wheel arrangement in the United States. In the late 1870s, Lehigh Valley was getting 22,400 miles a year out of locomotives like this, which was routinely used to haul trains moving 30 four-wheel cars of coal, each filled with 13,440 pounds of Pennsylvania anthracite. Notice how Baldwin renumbered this old wet plate to fit its revised photo numbering system by scratching out previous numbers and writing in 73 below the fourth set of drivers. *Baldwin image No. 73, courtesy H. L. Broadbelt Baldwin Collection (RR88.2), Railroad Museum of Pennsylvania (PHMC)*

its first engine in 1838 (to Cuba) and by the mid-1860s exported engines to a half-dozen countries. Over the next few decades, however, it would dramatically expand both the number of engines sold overseas and the list of nations to which it exported. While Baldwin had sold a few locomotives in Western Europe during its early years, among the largest new export markets it would develop were Central and South America, the Caribbean islands, Russia, New Zealand, and Japan.

Other new markets developed too, such as narrow gauge. Narrow gauge tracks allowed for railway construction to places

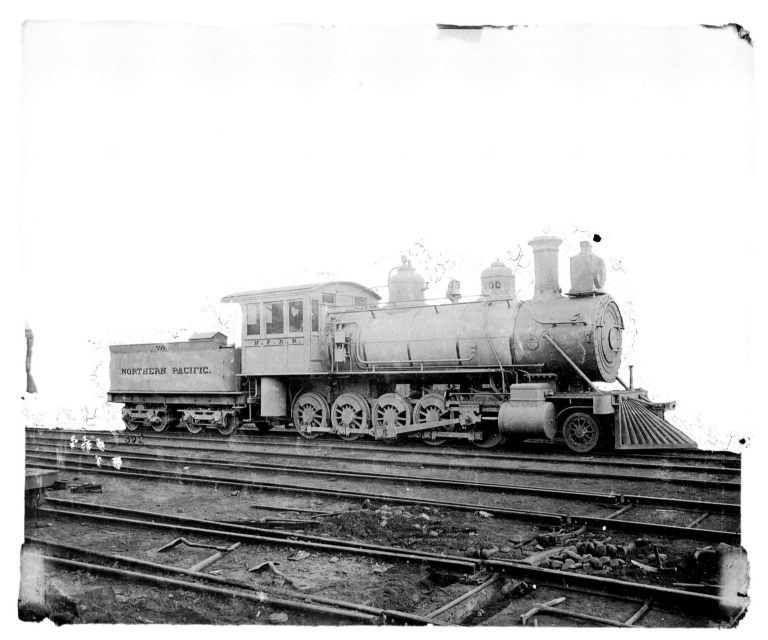

SPECIFICATIONS
Northern Pacific No. 500
Wheel arrangement: 2-10-0
Cylinders: Two 22x26 in.
Drivers: 45 in.
Total engine weight: 145,000 lbs.
Tractive effort: 34,800 lbs.

Northern Pacific No. 500 was one of two 2-10-0 Decapods that Baldwin built for NP in August 1883. It appears to have been painted in some color other than black—probably bluish, judging from the orthochromatic sensitivity of the plates. Although we tend to imagine that all locomotives from the coal-burning period were as black as their fuel, some were, in fact, dressed more colorfully. *Baldwin image No. 302, construction No. 8168, courtesy H. L. Broadbelt Baldwin Collection (RR88.2), Railroad Museum of Pennsylvania (PHMC)*

previously deemed uneconomical. Narrower tracks needed narrower rights-of-way, permitted smaller and cheaper equipment, and therefore didn't require the same degree of earthwork for cuts and fills, while allowing for tighter curvature. Baldwin sold its first narrow gauge locomotives in 1868 to West Virginia's Averill Coal & Oil Company. The following year, Baldwin built three narrow gauge locomotives for Brazil. In the American West, General William Jackson Palmer's Denver & Rio Grande had set an important precedent for narrow gauge lines. Baldwin built D&RG's first engine in 1871. The narrow gauge movement quickly gained momentum, and by the early 1870s narrow gauge railways were being planned and built all over the United States. John K. Brown, in his book *The Baldwin Locomotive Works 1831–1915*, points out that in the 1870s Baldwin commanded 45 percent of the narrow gauge locomotive market.

Little is known about Chimbote Railway's steam car *Emilia*, an unusual locomotive-powered passenger car that served as a railway inspection car or worked in branch-line passenger service. *Baldwin image No. 98, courtesy H. L. Broadbelt Baldwin Collection (RR88.2), Railroad Museum of Pennsylvania (PHMC)*

Initially, Baldwin had developed specialized types for narrow gauge operation. Warner describes these locomotives as follows:

[Passenger locomotives] were six-wheeled with four wheels coupled 40 inches in diameter, and 9 by 16-inch cylinders. They weighed each, loaded, about 25,000 pounds. [Freight locomotives] were eight-wheeled, with six wheels coupled, 36 inches in diameter, and 11 by 16-inch cylinders. These locomotives weighed each, loaded, about 35,000 lbs. Both types had a swinging truck with a single pair of wheels in front of the cylinders. The six-coupled design was for freight service, and was subsequently built in larger sizes. The four-coupled type for passenger service was found to be too small and to be unsteady on the track, owing to its comparatively short wheel base. It was therefore abandoned and the order American pattern, eight-wheeled, four-coupled, substituted.

As noted, Baldwin adapted the 2-8-0 Consolidation to narrow gauge service, and it first built three-foot-gauge 2-8-0s for D&RG in 1873. This type was used in both freight and passenger service and became a standard locomotive on the railroad's steeply graded Rocky Mountain lines.

SPECIFICATIONS
Denver & Rio Grande No. 88
Wheel arrangement: 4-4-0
Cylinders: Two 12x18 in.
Drivers: 45 in.
Total engine weight: 40,000 lbs.
Tractive effort: n/a

This image is among the oldest surviving wet-plate negatives in the Broadbelt Collection. It features Denver & Rio Grande three-foot-gauge 4-4-0 *Ptarmigan*, built in July 1880. We can only assume a great many early photographs were lost prior to Baldwin's adoption of its latter-day photo-numbering system. Notice the plate's original number has been scratched out. *Baldwin image No. 14, construction No. 5198, courtesy H. L. Broadbelt Baldwin Collection (RR88.2), Railroad Museum of Pennsylvania (PHMC)*

SPECIFICATIONS

New York Elevated No. 24

Wheel arrangement: 0-4-0T

Cylinders: Two 9x10 in.

Drivers: 34 in.

Total engine weight: 15,700 lbs.

Tractive effort: n/a

This 0-4-0T was built for the New York Elevated Railroad Company in 1878. A small, bidirectional tank engine, it features an unusually short wheelbase to negotiate very tight curves on the New York Els. Its reciprocating parts and drivers are substantially smaller than those on locomotives built for mainline service. Baldwin photographed this diminutive engine on September 14, 1878, using a collodion wet plate. *Baldwin image No. 124, construction No. 4431, courtesy H. L. Broadbelt Baldwin Collection (RR88.2), Railroad Museum of Pennsylvania (PHMC)*

Two other important areas of Baldwin diversification were small industrial locomotives and urban transit locomotives. Both were highly specialized designs with more conservative proportions than the large locomotives designed for intercity road service. Small industrial locomotives often required lighter axle weight and unusual loading-gauge requirements than road engines. Markets for these engines included factories, collieries, steel mills, quarries, and other sectors of the growing industrial economy.

Transit engines also had specialized requirements. Growth of cities had spurred development of extensive street railways and, beginning in the 1870s in New York City and Brooklyn, elevated rapid-transit lines.

At first, street railways used horse cars, but by the mid-1870s a requirement for lightweight, enclosed locomotives developed. These took several forms. Some locomotives were essentially power units driving a self-propelled passenger car. Since street trackage was very lightly built, the engines needed to conform to a very light axle weight while fitting inside of a small passenger car. A similar development was an enclosed engine, called a "dummy car," that was disguised to resemble a typical horse car of the period. The theory often put forward for this unusual design was they were less likely to frighten horses and other pack animals. Probably of equal importance was their ability to blend into existing traffic and avoid offending persons with sensitive aesthetical tastes who didn't approve of locomotives or street railways. Baldwin built a demonstrator dummy car in 1875 that made the rounds of American street railways in an effort to generate interest in this novel form. Dummy cars enjoyed a decade of interest prior to the advent of electric street railways that used trolley car technology as perfected by Frank Sprague.

New York City's elevated railways were a pioneer form of "heavy" rail—urban mass transit running on iron viaducts over the city streets. The first line was cable-operated, but these cars were quickly replaced with steam-hauled trains. Elevated trains had very specific motive power requirements. Axle loads were light but had to negotiate very tight curves, thereby requiring a short wheelbase. The engines worked relatively short runs, made frequent stops, and needed to maintain tight schedules. Despite their light axle weight and short wheelbase they required comparatively high tractive effort to haul trains of wooden passenger cars up steep gradients while getting up to speed rapidly between stations. To accommodate a lack of turning facilities, most transit locomotives were designed for bidirectional operation and to reverse directions quickly at terminals. One of the more innovative types to develop within these parameters was the Forney tank engine, which used the 0-4-4T wheel arrangement. This essentially comprised an engine and a fixed tender together on an extended frame. Placing most of the weight over driving wheels, and the fuel and water over a tender truck, minimized changes in engine weight distribution (and thus tractive effort) as supplies were depleted. By the end of the nineteenth century the electrification of New York's Els and similar elevated rapid transit lines in Chicago displaced the need for rapid transit steam locomotives.

Central R.R. of New Jersey June 1871

50

Central Railroad of New Jersey 2-4-4T No. 125, built June 1871, is a rare example of a bidirectional suburban locomotive built for an American railroad. CNJ, Illinois Central, New York Central, and a few other lines later operated bidirectional tank engines, but the type was an operational anomaly in American practice. However, in Britain, tank engines were quite common. Most famous of all the British tanks is the expressive light-blue locomotive featured in children's animation. The locomotive pictured here shares some characteristics with another animated locomotive made famous as "The Little Engine That Could." *Baldwin image No. 50, construction No. 2486, courtesy H. L. Broadbelt Baldwin Collection (RR88.2), Railroad Museum of Pennsylvania (PHMC)*

Baldwin's 20,000th locomotive was a prototype four-cylinder balanced compound designed by Samuel M. Vauclain and built in February 1902 for Florida's Plant System. The cylinders are arranged on a level plane, while two valve chambers (one for each side of the engine) are located above the cylinders. The photographer adjusted the large-format-plate camera to partially correct for distortion on the vertical plane, a common technique in architectural photography of the period. *Baldwin image No. 1652, construction No. 20000, courtesy H. L. Broadbelt Baldwin Collection (RR88.2), Railroad Museum of Pennsylvania (PHMC)*

CHAPTER **TWO**

COMPOUND LOCOMOTIVES

Opposite: Inquisitive Frenchmen inspect a Baldwin locomotive on display at the Paris Exposition of 1900. *Construction No. 17592, J. Yvor photograph, Railroad Museum of Pennsylvania (PHMC)*

IN THE RELATIVELY HIGH-PRESSURE locomotive engines built in the nineteenth century, considerable expansive power remained in the steam that was exhausted from the cylinders through the stack. One way to improve a steam engine's thermal efficiency was with a compound design that made more than one use of the steam's expansive power. When a compound does this with two sets of cylinders to expand steam twice, it is known as a double-expansion engine.

When operated correctly, a compound engine should require less steam to perform the same work as a simple engine, and thus burn less fuel and use less water. By one estimate, a properly functioning double-expansion compound locomotive may consume up to 20 percent less fuel and 50 percent less water than a simple locomotive of equivalent design. In actual service, the efficiency of a compound locomotive varied depending on the type of service and operating speed, as well as the skill of the engineer.

In a typical nineteenth-century compound locomotive engine, steam entered the high-pressure cylinder at roughly 180 pounds per square inch (psi) and was exhausted into the low-pressure cylinder at roughly 60 to 80 psi, where it expanded again before finally exhausting through the stack at approximately 5 to 20 psi. To balance the thrust, the low-pressure cylinder had a diameter two to three times that of the high-pressure cylinder.

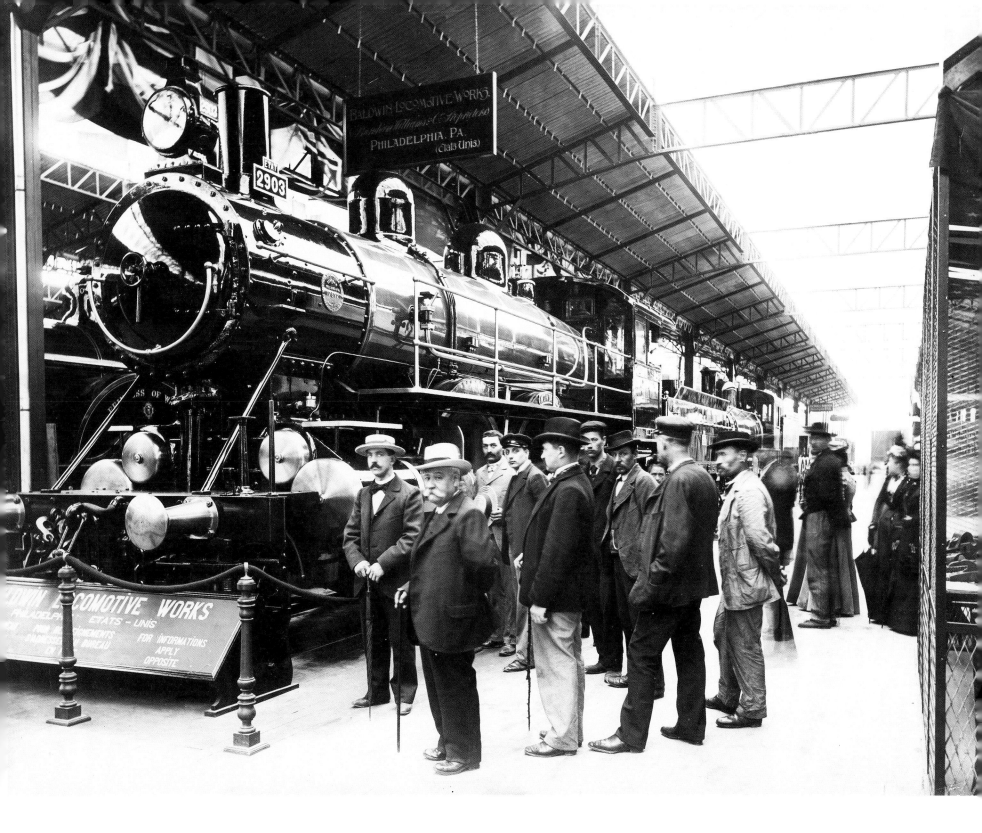

The concept of a compound steam engine had been around for a long time, predating the locomotive itself by several decades. The first documented compound was designed by Jonathan Hornblower in Britain in 1781. A generation passed before the concept was tried again, this time by Arthur Woolf, who refined and perfected a compound engine in 1804. Despite these formative efforts, many more years passed before the concept gained acceptance, and it was longer still before the design was adapted to a practical locomotive in America.

COMPOUND LOCOMOTIVES IN AMERICA

One of the earliest applications of the compound design to a locomotive in the United States was a little-known tandem compound built by the Shepard Iron Works in Buffalo, New York, in the 1860s. This curious machine was constructed from the parts of an earlier locomotive. Like many pioneers, it established a precedent but is not understood to have directly influenced future compound development. It really wasn't until the late 1880s, when railroads were seeking improved fuel efficiency and better locomotive performance, that compound types gained a commercial foothold.

Faced with growing traffic and ever higher fuel bills, railroads sought greater power and efficiency in the late nineteenth century. Compounds were especially attractive to lines that suffered from a dearth of adequate water, such as railroads crossing the western deserts. Compounds offered other advantages too, such as moving more tonnage with a single locomotive, thus making the engine crew more productive.

Positive operating characteristics intrinsic to compound designs also contributed to their efficiency. For example, a compound produced a gentler firebox draft. While draft is key to a locomotive's operation when it is starting or working hard at full throttle (exhaust from cylinders draws air across the fire, causing it to burn hotter, thus allowing greater steaming capacity as the engine gains speed), the violent draft in a simple engine tended to force voluminous clouds of cinders and unburned coal through the stack. Not only did this waste fuel, it soiled the environment, causing complaints from enginemen, passengers, and

people along the line. Heavy grades where locomotives worked especially hard were covered in blankets of cinders and coal dust that marked the land and fouled ballast (which impaired drainage and damaged the track bed). Since compounding steam lessened the force of the draft, these engines spewed less firebox material out the stack. Marshall M. Kirkman in his 1899 book, *The Compound Locomotive*, notes that a compound's "milder exhaust and consequently . . . slower rate of combustion produces a greater evaporation of water per pound of fuel."

Despite efficiency gains, compound locomotives suffered notable defects. By nature of its design, a compound was a more complicated machine. It required more moving parts, involved more complex steam connections, or both. More and heavier moving parts added to reciprocating weight, requiring more lubrication and more intensive maintenance. Furthermore, to achieve the theoretical rates of efficiency, proper operation of a compound was crucial. Some of the more common complaints from railroads included difficulties in training engineers to work them in the most efficient manner.

Several different configurations of compound locomotives were built in the United States. Baldwin was a leading producer of these types for several decades.

TWO-CYLINDER COMPOUNDS

Among the first successful double-expansion locomotives were two-cylinder cross compounds, first developed in Germany in 1887 and soon constructed by various builders in the United States. A cross compound features a high-pressure cylinder on one side of the locomotive, which exhausts into a low-pressure cylinder on the other. Despite the unbalanced appearance, carefully balancing the output of low- and high-pressure cylinders allowed the cross compound to work reasonably well in slow-speed service.

Of the early commercial applications in the United States, Baldwin's competitor Schenectady Locomotive Works' design was best known. This was the work of Albert Pitkin and was sold beginning in 1889. In the last decade of the nineteenth century, variations of cross compounds were designed by a number of builders, including Baldwin. These designs principally differed in

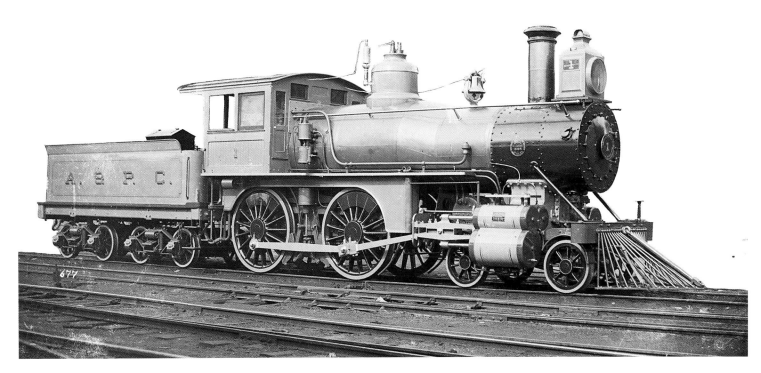

SPECIFICATIONS
Altoona & Pittsburgh No. 1
Wheel arrangement: 4-4-0
High-pressure cylinders: Two 12x24 in.
Low-pressure cylinders: Two 20x24 in.
Drivers: 68 in.
Total engine weight: n/a
Tractive effort: n/a

Samuel M. Vauclain's 1889 patent for a four-cylinder compound specified that a 4-4-0 American type could easily be converted to compound operation. At the time of his patent filing, the 4-4-0 still reigned supreme as the most common type on American railroads. However, as the Vauclain compound gained favor, new passenger wheel arrangements came into vogue, and relatively few 4-4-0s, compared with other wheel arrangements, were equipped as Vauclains. This brightly colored locomotive was built in 1892 for Altoona & Pittsburgh Connecting Railroad. *Baldwin image No. 00677, construction No. 13804, courtesy H. L. Broadbelt Baldwin Collection (RR88.2), Railroad Museum of Pennsylvania (PHMC)*

the types and arrangements of starting valves, often described as interceptor valves. This equipment enabled the engineer to work a compound locomotive as a simple engine. Although an engine achieved maximum efficiency as a compound, in circumstances like starting a heavy train, maximum power was necessary, so it was advantageous to run the locomotive as a simple engine for short periods.

While Schenectady and its corporate successor, Alco, represent the most significant proponent of the cross-compound type, Baldwin began building them in 1892. Kirkman notes that Baldwin's early efforts were known as "automatic compounds" because Baldwin's starting valve allowed the engines to start with high-pressure steam to both cylinders. After the first couple of piston strokes, they automatically cut over to compound operation.

This ensured that the engine achieved the economic advantages of compound operation as soon as possible, however, it impaired the engineer's operational flexibility, limiting the ability of the engine, and it was ultimately dispensed with in favor of a valve that allowed the engineer to switch from simple to compound at will. Baldwin's Samuel M. Vauclain was awarded a patent on a two-cylinder type in 1893. Despite this, Baldwin built relatively few cross compounds in comparison with other types.

VAUCLAIN COMPOUND

Far more significant to Baldwin's production was the four-cylinder compound designed by Vauclain. This proved to be one of the most distinctive and successful varieties of compound locomotive and was generally known by its inventor's name.

This schematic depicts one side of a Vauclain compound to show the relationship of the high-pressure (A) and low-pressure (B) cylinders to the piston valve (V), as well as the flow of steam. Dark blue indicates high-pressure steam flowing from the boiler, purple indicates steam having done its work in the high-pressure cylinder flowing to the low-pressure cylinder, and light blue indicates very low-pressure steam being exhausted into the atmosphere. High-pressure piston (R) drives piston rod (r), while low-pressure piston (Q) drives piston rod (q). Both piston rods are connected to a common crosshead (not pictured). Piston valve (V) slides back and forth in the opposite direction as the pistons to admit and release steam from both cylinders. International Textbook Company, *A Textbook on the Locomotive and the Airbrake, Richard Jay Solomon collection*

Right: This line drawing shows the two common Vauclain compound cylinders and valve chamber arrangements. (A) is the high-pressure cylinder, (B) is the low-pressure cylinder, and (C) is the valve chamber. Cylinder orientation varied depending on drive-wheel diameter as well as lateral clearance considerations along the intended line of operation. International Textbook Company, *A Textbook on the Locomotive and the Airbrake, Richard Jay Solomon collection*

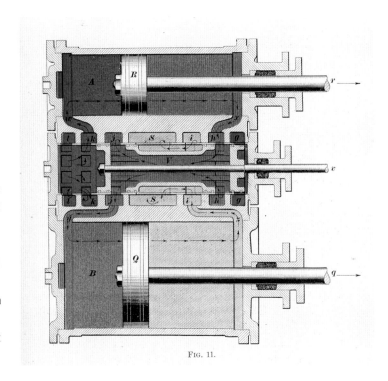

FIG. 11.

Vauclain patented this type in 1889, and Baldwin built the first commercial Vauclain compound for Baltimore & Ohio in October of that year. In the specifications for the design, Vauclain described his innovation in letters dated June 25, 1889, and filed February 21, 1889, for United States Patent 406,011:

> *The objective of my invention is to construct a compound locomotive-engine in which both the high and low pressure cylinders are on the same side of the locomotive, side by side, and connected to a common cross-head, so that an equal amount of power is delivered to each side of the engine, a further object being to so construct the parts that a locomotive of the single-acting American type can be readily altered into a compound locomotive.*

The high- and low-pressure cylinders were located directly above one another on each side of the engine, while the specific arrangement of the cylinders depended on the space allowed and varied depending on the specific application. Locomotives with high drivers, such as passenger locomotives, typically featured low-pressure cylinders below the high-pressure cylinders, while locomotives with very low drivers, or those facing other restrictions, featured high-pressure cylinders below to accommodate tight clearances.

Cylinders were cast as a single piece that also incorporated a cylindrical valve chamber. Vauclain's design was among the earliest to incorporate cylindrical piston valves in place of the more conventional slide valves. Kirkman notes that piston valves offered superior valve and port arrangements that were suited to the more complex steam passages of the four-cylinder compound. These valves were a double-ended hollow design, and one valve on each side of the engine was used to govern steam admission and exhaust to high- and low-pressure cylinders. This required an unusually complicated network of steam passages in the valve chamber as well as the valve. Complex steam passages allowed for simple valve motion and other equipment that greatly contributed to the success of Vauclain's design.

The cylindrical piston valve was a significant innovation. At the time Vauclain incorporated it in his design, this valve was relatively unusual. More than a decade later, the advantages of

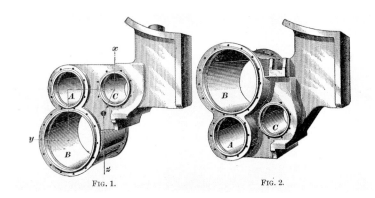

FIG. 1.   FIG. 2.

the piston valve (especially its ease of lubrication) resulted in its general adoption. Ultimately, the piston valve superseded slide valve designs that had been standard since the early days of the American locomotive.

The Vauclain compound offered a number of advantages. Except for its dual pairs of cylinders, in most respects it used the same configuration as a conventional simple steam engine. Other than its valve arrangement, it did not use a host of complex equipment, nor was it fitted with reciprocating parts that were difficult to counterbalance. As noted in the patent, an intended benefit of this simplicity was the ease of application to an existing locomotive. Kirkman also notes that packing rings, bushings, and valves were more easily repaired and replaced. Operation of the locomotive was aided by an arrangement of cylinders that was more balanced than the arrangement used by cross compounds. Specifically, this caused fewer stresses as a result of side-to-side imbalances. Frank M. Swengel notes that the balanced system avoided the "racking" action associated with two-cylinder

Built in 1899, Wabash 4-4-0 No. 659 features an unusual clerestory cab roof that was ordered on many of this railroad's locomotives during the 1890s. Wabash deemed itself the "Banner Route," and while this engine appears gray in the photo, it may have been painted a more lively color. This American type served for three decades and was scrapped in 1933. *Baldwin image No. 1214, construction No. 16918, courtesy H. L. Broadbelt Baldwin Collection (RR88.2), Railroad Museum of Pennsylvania (PHMC)*

The 2-6-2 Prairie type briefly ran as a fast passenger engine early in the twentieth century. Santa Fe's first Prairie, No. 1000, is pictured here. This is a Vauclain compound from 1901 with 79-inch drivers—then the epitome of a modern locomotive. Problems at speed discouraged further development of the 2-6-2 as a passenger locomotive, although Santa Fe and others later adopted it for freight work. Two decades after these 2-6-2s were built, Santa Fe rebuilt them with smaller drivers and converted them to simple operation. *Construction No. 19578, courtesy H. L. Broadbelt Baldwin Collection (RR88.2), Railroad Museum of Pennsylvania (PHMC)*

compounds. As a result, the Vauclain system enjoyed greater versatility and could be applied to faster services.

To minimize difficulties caused by back pressure in the low-pressure cylinder at higher speeds, Vauclain compounds often used larger driving wheels than comparable simple locomotives. Larger wheels reduced the number of piston strokes necessary to reach any given speed. To overcome back-pressure difficulties further, the cutoff was shortened, which limited steam admission to the cylinders during the course of the piston stroke. As a result of these adjustments, in the 1890s a number of railroads (including Reading Company, Lehigh Valley, and Burlington)

bought Vauclains for fast passenger service, although, generally speaking, simple engines were better suited to fast service and Vauclain compounds were not as efficient at higher speeds as they were when worked more conservatively.

Like the other compound designs of the period, Vauclains were equipped with a starting valve to enable the engineer to operate the locomotive as a simple engine during starting or at other times when greater power was necessary, such as working a heavy grade at very slow speeds.

To get the engine moving, high-pressure steam was admitted to low-pressure cylinders for the first couple of strokes. In his

SPECIFICATIONS
Atlantic City Railroad No. 1027
Wheel arrangement: 4-4-2
High-pressure cylinders: Two 13x26 in.
Low-pressure cylinders: Two 22x26 in.
Drivers: 84¼ in.
Total engine weight: 142,900 lbs.
Tractive effort: 14,400 lbs.

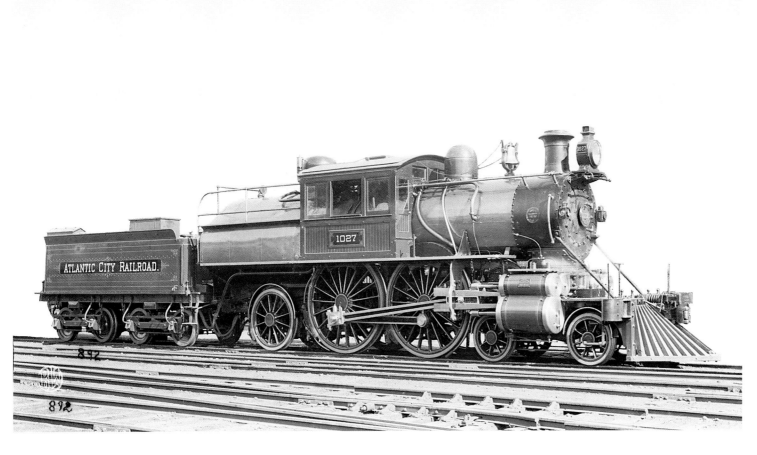

Atlantic City Railroad was part of the Philadelphia & Reading system. Locomotive 1027 was among the earliest Atlantic types, named not for the ACR but rather for the Atlantic Coast Line, which was first to try this wheel arrangement. ACR's famous Vauclain compound was one of two built for the line in March 1896. These had 84¼-inch driving wheels—among the tallest used on an American engine—and were known for fast running. In 1897, the type would typically sprint across New Jersey averaging more than 60 miles per hour between stops on the Atlantic City run. Its success spurred interest in the new type as a fast passenger locomotive. *Baldwin image No. 00892, construction No. 14740, courtesy H. L. Broadbelt Baldwin Collection (RR88.2), Railroad Museum of Pennsylvania (PHMC)*

manuscript entitled *Compound Locomotives*, Paul T. Warner explains that "the effective pressure was much greater on the low-pressure piston than on the high-pressure, so that in starting the locomotive the low-pressure cylinder did most of the work."

Once the train was started, the engineer would switch back to compound operation. To ensure greatest efficiency, it was important to switch to compound as soon as possible. On Vauclain compounds, the starting valve was sometimes known as a bypass valve because it did not use the interceptor arrangement found on the two-cylinder compounds.

Among the disadvantages inherent to the type, as Warner notes, was that the high-pressure starting arrangement "tended to throw the cross-heads out of line, resulting in excessive wear to the cross-heads and guides, not to mention frequent trouble due to leaking piston rod packing." This required more careful lubrication of these components and regular inspection and maintenance. As larger locomotives were developed using the Vauclain system, these inherent defects became more pronounced.

The Vauclain was built in a great variety of wheel arrangements, perhaps more than any other type of American compound

SPECIFICATIONS

Philadelphia & Reading No. 378

Wheel arrangement: 4-2-2

High-pressure cylinders: Two 13x26 in.

Low-pressure cylinders: Two 22x26 in.

Drivers: 84¼ in.

Total engine weight: 122,000 lbs.

Tractive effort: 14,400 lbs.

This remarkable Philadelphia & Reading photograph was exposed on a 12x20-inch glass plate. It depicts P&R bicycle-type Vauclain compound No. 378 leading a Philadelphia–New York express passenger train at Reading Terminal in 1896. According to George M. Hart, in his youth Paul T. Warner (later Baldwin's librarian) was afforded a cab ride on this unusual Baldwin engine and retained a copy of this photograph in his personal archive. This image was published in the April 1923 *Baldwin Locomotives* as part of a detailed history of Reading steam power. *Philadelphia & Reading photograph by Henry Harmer, courtesy George M. Hart Collection (RR2005.39), Railroad Museum of Pennsylvania (PHMC)*

design. The earliest Vauclains were 4-4-0s, but the type was later adapted to 2-6-0, 4-6-0, 4-4-2, 2-8-0, and 2-6-2 arrangements, as well as some curious high-speed wheel arrangements, such as the 2-4-2 Columbia and experimental 4-2-2s built for the Reading. In addition, some locomotives were built with the Vauclain system for the Manitou & Pikes Peak Railway that used the Abt rack system for ascending grades up to 25 percent (a 1 foot rise for every 4 feet traveled).

In his book, *The Baldwin Locomotive Works*, John K. Brown notes that by 1900, 70 percent of all the compounds built in the United States were of the Vauclain type. Baldwin exported large numbers of Vauclains, selling them in Russia, Japan, France, and Germany.

TANDEM COMPOUNDS

The four-cylinder tandem compound was an early experimental double-expansion type. A Boston & Albany locomotive was equipped with this arrangement in about 1883, however, the first truly successful application was the result of refinement by the Brooks Locomotive Works in 1892.

The tandem compound was defined by a pair of cylinders on each side of the locomotive, with the high-pressure cylinders directly ahead of the low-pressure cylinders. The high- and low-pressure cylinders were mounted end to end and connected to a common piston rod. As with the Vauclain system, one piston valve on each side of the engine controlled steam admission for both high- and low-pressure cylinders. The tandem compound offered even more thrust than the cross compound, and in service it was viewed more favorably because the use of common crosshead and piston rods was deemed superior to more complex arrangements used by other four-cylinder compound types. Most tandem compounds were conceived as heavy-freight haulers.

Warner writes, "The tandem design was preferable to the Vauclain in that there was less tendency to wear the guides and crossheads." Although it offered a number of advantages, the tandem type suffered from several distinctive failings. Both

SPECIFICATIONS
Baltimore & Ohio No. 1940
Wheel arrangement: 2-8-0
High-pressure cylinders: Two 15½x30 in.
Low-pressure cylinders: Two 26x30 in.
Drivers: 54 in.
Total engine weight: n/a
Tractive effort: n/a

Vauclain compounds with low driving wheels, such as this Baltimore & Ohio 2-8-0 built for heavy freight service, tended to have the low-pressure cylinders above the high-pressure cylinders for clearance reasons. B&O No. 1940 was completed in July 1900, and this Baldwin image was retouched to clean up the appearance of the engine. *Construction No. 17978, courtesy H. L. Broadbelt Baldwin Collection (RR88.2), Railroad Museum of Pennsylvania (PHMC)*

Warner and Swengel note that difficulties tended to develop in the packing between the high- and low-pressure cylinders, and routine maintenance was more complicated because access to the low-pressure cylinder required removal of the high-pressure assembly. Perhaps more significant was the greater reciprocating weight incurred by the four-cylinder arrangement, resulting in difficult counterbalancing arrangements. For this reason, tandem compounds were better suited to slower services where reciprocating forces were less severe.

The Santa Fe Railway was one of the more enthusiastic customers for tandem compounds, buying a large number from Baldwin beginning in 1902. Unique to Santa Fe were

SPECIFICATIONS

Columbia

Wheel arrangement: 2-4-2

High-pressure cylinders: Two 13x26 in.

Low-pressure cylinders: Two 22x26 in.

Drivers: 84¼ in.

Total engine weight: 126,640 lbs.

Tractive effort: n/a

Baldwin's *Columbia* was an experimental Vauclain compound locomotive used to demonstrate the advantages of the 2-4-2 wheel arrangement for high-speed passenger service. It was so named because it was displayed at the 1893 Columbia Exposition in Chicago. *Baldwin image No. 703, construction No. 13350, courtesy H. L. Broadbelt Baldwin Collection (RR88.2), Railroad Museum of Pennsylvania (PHMC)*

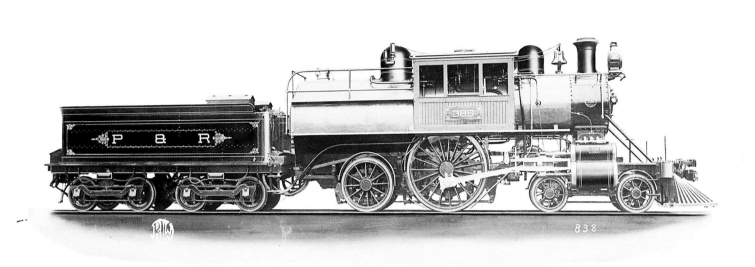

its exceptionally large 2-10-2 tandems built by both Alco and Baldwin for the railway's freight services. The 2-10-2 wheel arrangement was known as the Santa Fe type because the railroad was the first to adapt it successfully.

DEGLEHN AND BALANCED COMPOUNDS

Frenchman Alfred G. DeGlehn began building four-cylinder compounds in 1886. As he refined his designs, his four-cylinder, four-crank "balanced compounds" found considerable popularity in Europe before catching the attention of engineers around the world, eventually including American railroads in the early twentieth century. The basic arrangement that distinguishes this type includes four cylinders in a horizontal line and four crank points instead of two.

Typically, two high-pressure cylinders are located inside the locomotive frames and power the lead driving wheels using a cranked axle, while low-pressure cylinders are located outside the frame in the conventional position and use external rods connected to outside crank pins on a second set of drive wheels in the familiar pattern.

In 1904, the Pennsylvania Railroad imported a state-of-the-art DeGlehn compound with a 4-4-2 wheel arrangement from French builder Société Alsacienne de Construction Mécaniques, while New York Central worked with Alco to adapt the DeGlehn design on an experimental 4-4-2. Baldwin's Samuel M. Vauclain adapted the balanced type for domestic applications. Like the Vauclain compound previously described, Baldwin's newer four-cylinder balanced type used

SPECIFICATIONS
Manitou & Pikes Peak No. 5
Wheel arrangement: 0-4-2T rack engine
High-pressure cylinders: Two 10x22 in.
Low-pressure cylinders: Two 25x22 in.
Drivers: 22½ in.
Total engine weight: n/a
Tractive effort: n/a

Colorado's Manitou & Pikes Peak ordered several unusual Vauclain compounds equipped for the Abt rack system for climbing exceptionally steep gradients. This one was tested at Baldwin on April 20, 1901. Today, some of the only surviving Vauclain compounds are of this type, since in the early years of the twentieth century most of the road-service Vauclains were either converted to simple operation or scrapped. This locomotive is preserved at Manitou, Colorado. *Baldwin image No. 1468, construction No. 18935, courtesy H. L. Broadbelt Baldwin Collection (RR88.2), Railroad Museum of Pennsylvania (PHMC)*

a common piston valve for respective high- and low-pressure cylinders. This was set in a position between the two cylinders slightly above the cylinders' centerline. Where the French balanced compound featured central cylinder heads placed noticeably forward from the heads of the outside cylinders, Baldwin's balanced-design cylinder heads were all in a line.

Contributing to better balance was the improved piston arrangement made possible by the cranked axle that allowed for parallel high- and low-pressure pistons traveling in opposite directions from one another, compared with the Vauclain type on which cylinders on the same side moved back and forth together. Improved reciprocating balance overcame many of the difficulties associated with the Vauclain compound. The type also benefited from having twice as many impulses per driving wheel revolution as other types. Where other types of locomotives had just two crankpins set 180 degrees apart,

the balanced compound had four crank positions set 90 degrees apart. This required less torque for each stroke and produced less strain on drive rods and related parts while helping to offset reciprocating weight. Swengel notes there were still some minor inequities in weight, since the drive rods connecting the outside cylinders with the rear drive wheels were longer than those used to reach the cranked axle, and the high- and low-pressure cylinders were still of different sizes. As a result, Baldwin built few

SPECIFICATIONS
Pennsylvania Railroad No. 2759
Wheel arrangement: 4-4-2
High-pressure cylinders: Two 16x26 in.
Low-pressure cylinders: Two 27x26 in.
Drivers: 80 in.
Total engine weight: n/a
Tractive effort: n/a

Pennsylvania Railroad Class E28 Atlantic was an experimental locomotive built in April 1905 as a Baldwin balanced compound. In 1903–1904 Pennsylvania Railroad imported a similarly designed DeGlehn compound from France. Despite these experiments, PRR was not enthralled with the compound concept and preferred conventional simple locomotive designs. *Baldwin image No. 01985, construction No. 25548, courtesy H. L. Broadbelt Baldwin Collection (RR88.2), Railroad Museum of Pennsylvania (PHMC)*

This 4-4-2 balanced compound 2997 was one of six Baldwin built in 1901 for the French railway Compagnie des Chemins de Fer Paris à Lyon à la Méditerranée—known commonly as P.L.M. Although American railroads largely abandoned the compound concept early in the twentieth century, French railways continued to refine and perfect compound steam locomotive design into the 1950s. *Baldwin image No. 1407, construction No. 18528, courtesy H. L. Broadbelt Baldwin Collection (RR88.2), Railroad Museum of Pennsylvania (PHMC)*

Vauclains after introduction of the four-cylinder balanced type. An article in the October 1903 issue of *Railway and Locomotive Engineering* conveyed the comments of Baldwin's Mr. McCarroll on the benefits of the four-cylinder balanced compound:

1. *Practically a perfect balanced locomotive.*
2. *Lightness of reciprocating parts.*
3. *Smoothness in running.*
4. *Quickness in starting and handling trains.*
5. *Reduction of injury to track and permanent way structures.*
6. *The usual advantages claimed for compound locomotives (economy in fuel and water).*

Despite these claims, the type had its failings and only enjoyed a few years of interest in the United States. One of its drawbacks was increased maintenance costs incurred by the interior cylinders; many railroads determined that these costs negated any potential savings from improved efficiency. Furthermore,

the type was introduced about the same time as superheating, which effectively ended interest in non-articulated compounds.

DECLINE OF THE NON-ARTICULATED COMPOUND

Non-articulated compounds rapidly fell out of favor in the early years of the twentieth century, largely as a result of the practical development of superheating combined with a move toward faster services for which many compounds were ill suited. Superheating achieved much of the same efficiency of compounding without complicated equipment. It was noted that when railroads failed to keep their more complex compound types in perfect running order, the engine's overall efficiency sagged significantly. Furthermore, the efficiency gains offered by compounds in general were offset by disadvantages associated with more complicated operation and more difficult maintenance requirements. Consider this item published in the August 1902 issue of *Railway and Locomotive Engineering*, which, in a discussion about the cost of moving freight and compounds, relayed these opinions of an unnamed railroad president:

> *[T]his president, who exercises very great authority and is a close observer of every detail of railroad operating [sic], proceeded to denounce compound locomotives in the most vigorous terms. He did not regard the saving of a few pounds of coal per train mile as being of any consequence, compared with regularity of service, and he knew that compound locomotives spend much more time undergoing repairs than those of simple build. On that account he would have no more compound locomotives built for his system. When a compound locomotive missed a trip undergoing repairs and when it failed on the road, both of which happened frequently, he said, the loss to the company was greater than a gain from coal saving would amount to in a year.*

SPECIFICATIONS
Great Northern No. 1700
Wheel arrangement: 4-4-2
High-pressure cylinders: Two 15x26 in.
Low-pressure cylinders: Two 25x26 in.
Drivers: 73 in.
Total engine weight: n/a
Tractive effort: n/a

Great Northern No.1700 was built as a balanced compound in April 1906 and had its official portrait created in May of that year. It operated with 210-psi boiler pressure. The high-pressure cylinders were located inside the frames and powered the first pair of drive wheels using a cranked axle, while the low-pressure outside cylinders were connected to the rear pair of drivers. The arrangement didn't please GN, and after a few years locomotives of this type were rebuilt as simple engines. *Baldwin image No. 2168, construction No. 28037, courtesy H. L. Broadbelt Baldwin Collection (RR88.2), Railroad Museum of Pennsylvania (PHMC)*

It appears that this president was not alone in his sentiments. Another issue affecting compounds involved changes to service requirements: many compound designs were intended for slow-speed freight service, and as railroads moved to faster freight services, these slow-speed types became less desirable.

Non-articulated compound locomotives attained their greatest popularity in the 1890s, and interest peaked in the early years of the twentieth century. Alfred Bruce, an Alco engineer in the 1950s and author of *The Steam Locomotive in America*, estimated that in 1904 just 2,884 locomotives had been built as compounds, representing roughly 6 percent of the national total. This was the same year that the articulated Mallet compound was introduced to American service. Very few non-articulated compounds were built after 1907, and many locomotives built as compounds were converted to simple operation.

MALLET ARTICULATED

In 1874, Swiss inventor Anatole Mallet (pronounced *MAL-lay*) was granted a French patent for an articulated compound locomotive that effectively placed two engines under a common boiler using an articulated frame to negotiate tight curvature. The forward engine could swing laterally while continuing to support the front portion of the boiler. The Mallet was among the earliest commercially successful compound locomotive types and was first

SPECIFICATIONS
Santa Fe No. 1251
Wheel arrangement: 4-6-2
High-pressure cylinders: Two 17x28 in.
Low-pressure cylinders: Two 28x28 in.
Drivers: 73 in.
Total engine weight: 151,900 lbs.
Tractive effort: 32,800 lbs.

Santa Fe traversed hundreds of miles across the arid Southwest, where water was scarce, and what little there was often contained minerals harmful to boilers. As a result, Santa Fe was very interested in water conservation. No. 1252 is a balanced compound, one of 41 Class 1226 Pacifics Baldwin built in 1905 and 1906 for Santa Fe passenger service. *Construction No. 26533, courtesy H. L. Broadbelt Baldwin Collection (RR88.2), Railroad Museum of Pennsylvania (PHMC)*

With their headlights covered, Great Northern's first five Class L-1 2-6-6-2s await shipping west at Philadelphia in 1906. Regarding his sale of the first 2-6-6-2 Mallets to GN, Vauclain recalled his conversation with James J. Hill in his 1926 biography, *Steaming Up!*: "We can't sell you just one big Mallet. . . . If we sold you one it would be passed from one division master mechanic to another, each one glad to get rid of it. You know the average railroader will shy at novelties. You should buy five Mallets for service on the Cascades Mountains at Skykomish where the grade is 2.2 percent and short curves are combined with tunnels and plenty of snowsheds." *Baldwin image No. 02648, courtesy H. L. Broadbelt Baldwin Collection (RR88.2), Railroad Museum of Pennsylvania (PHMC)*

applied to European narrow gauge lines where tight curvature precluded operation of engines with long wheelbases, and where steep gradients demanded locomotives with great tractive effort.

Baltimore & Ohio's president, Leonor F. Loree, developed a fascination with articulated locomotives. In the early years of the twentieth century he requested that B&O's general superintendent of motive power, John E. Muhlfeld, develop an experimental articulated. Muhlfeld worked with engineering forces at the recently formed American Locomotive Company (Alco) in

adapting the Mallet to American road-freight service as a pusher engine. In 1903–1904, Alco's Schenectady Works built America's first Mallet for B&O. The resulting technological hybrid was new to American rails, although the articulated design drew comparisons with Fairlie types bought by some American narrow gauge lines. Yet, where the Fairlies and European Mallets had been designed to give narrow gauge lines greater power, Alco's Mallet was scaled for heavy standard gauge freight service, and was by far the heaviest locomotive ever built.

SPECIFICATIONS
American Railroad of Porto Rico No. 35

Wheel arrangement: 0-6-6-0
High-pressure cylinders: Two 12½x20 in.
Low-pressure cylinders: Two 19x20 in.
Drivers: 36 in.
Total engine weight: 106,650 lbs.
Tractive effort: n/a

Shortly after Alco debuted its pioneer Mallet—Baltimore & Ohio No. 2400—Baldwin constructed a three-meter-gauge 0-6-6-0 Mallet for the American Railroad of Porto Rico [*sic*]. Locomotive No. 35 was completed in November 1904. *Baldwin image No. 01938, construction No. 24827, courtesy H. L. Broadbelt Baldwin Collection (RR88.2), Railroad Museum of Pennsylvania (PHMC)*

1938

BALDWIN LOCOMOTIVE WORKS.

SPECIFICATIONS

GN Class L-1

Wheel arrangement: 2-6-6-2

High-pressure cylinders: Two 21½x32 in.

Low-pressure cylinders: Two 33x32 in.

Drivers: 55 in.

Total engine weight: 355,000 lbs.

Tractive effort: 69,000 lbs.

When Baldwin's Samuel L. Vauclain secured an order for five 2-6-6-2s from Great Northern in 1906, they represented the first to use this wheel arrangement. Known on GN as Class L-1, they proved their merit, and GN bought many more of Mallet types, which eventually became one of the most popular compound designs built in the United States. *Construction No. 26601, courtesy H. L. Broadbelt Baldwin Collection (RR88.2), Railroad Museum of Pennsylvania (PHMC)*

Shortly after Alco's pioneer adaptation of the Mallet, Baldwin built an order for three-meter-gauge 0-6-6-0s for use by the "American Railroad of Porto Rico" [*sic*]. These were the first narrow gauge Mallets built in the United States and the first of the type built by Baldwin. In 1906, Baldwin designed a modified Mallet type, delivering five 2-6-6-2s to James J. Hill's Great Northern for road service in the Washington Cascades. These were the first Mallets designed to lead mainline freights, and also the first Mallets using the Belpaire firebox. Great Northern was one of a few railroads that preferred the boxy Belpaire firebox over the more common radial-stay design used by most American railroads.

GN placed repeat orders for 2-6-6-2s, giving it an additional 45 Baldwin Mallets by 1908. Alco and B&O were first to adapt the Mallet, but Baldwin and Great Northern established the type as a successful American road locomotive. The 2-6-6-2 became the most common wheel arrangement for domestic Mallet compounds. Most were built with relatively small driving wheels,

usually just 56 inches in diameter and designed to operate about 20 miles per hour in road service.

CAB-FORWARD

Southern Pacific watched GN's application of Mallet road locomotives carefully. Like Great Northern, SP faced unusually difficult mountain crossings. In 1909, Baldwin developed the new 2-8-8-2 Mallet for Southern Pacific's Donner Pass crossing of

SPECIFICATIONS

Southern Pacific No. 4000

Wheel arrangement: 2-8-8-2

High-pressure cylinders: Two 26x30 in.

Low-pressure cylinders: Two 40x30 in.

Drivers: 57 in.

Total engine weight: 394,150 lbs.

Tractive effort: 94,800 lbs.

Built in 1909, Southern Pacific's initial 2-8-8-2s were the first two locomotives with this new wheel arrangement. When SP encountered difficulties operating the locomotives in high-altitude snowshed territory on Donner Pass, it worked with Baldwin to reverse the orientation of the Mallet compound and in so doing created one of the most distinctive locomotive arrangements in North America. *Construction No. 33340, courtesy H. L. Broadbelt Baldwin Collection (RR88.2), Railroad Museum of Pennsylvania (PHMC)*

SPECIFICATIONS

Southern Pacific No. 4004

Wheel arrangement: 2-8-8-2

High-pressure cylinders: Two 26x30 in.

Low-pressure cylinders: Two 40x30 in.

Drivers: 57 in.

Total engine weight: 394,700 lbs.

Tractive effort: 94,880 lbs.

Southern Pacific's second order of 2-8-8-2s consisted of its first "cab-forwards," a type that became one of the railroad's trademark locomotives. In October 1909, SP Class MC-2 (Mallet Consolidation) No. 4004 is ready for shipping west. Like the railroad's first 2-8-8-2 Mallets, the second order used 26x30-inch high-pressure cylinders and 40x30-inch low-pressure cylinders. An interesting feature of this type was that the low-pressure cylinders remained at the smokebox end of the locomotive. *Construction No. 34044, courtesy H. L. Broadbelt Baldwin Collection (RR88.2), Railroad Museum of Pennsylvania (PHMC)*

the California Sierra. This pioneer application of the 2-8-8-2 arrangement was intended as much to reduce axle loadings by distributing locomotive weight over more driving wheels as to increase tractive effort.

SP classed its 2-8-8-2s as MC-1 (Mallet Consolidations). Although conventionally oriented locomotives, these resulted in one of the most distinctive locomotive variations built in the United States. During early trials on Donner, SP found that the massive machines suffered from excessive smoke.

This presented a serious problem when operating through Donner's long wooden sheds and tunnels. Not only did crews find it difficult to breathe, but at times it was nearly impossible to see. This situation threatened to make Mallet operation over Donner Pass unworkable. Unwilling to forgo obvious economic advantages of Mallet compounds on its busiest line, SP decided the best way to take advantage of Mallets on Donner was to turn the engines around. This unorthodox approach had been tried around the turn of

Southern Pacific's second fleet of cab-forward Mallets consisted of 12 Class MM-2s using the 2-6-6-2 wheel arrangement. Built by Baldwin in 1911, these were assigned to passenger services on Donner Pass. Difficulties with the leading pony truck soon led SP to rebuild the type with four-wheel leading trucks. This rare photo shows No. 1211 in its as-built condition, leading train No. 4 on Donner. Notice the staff-exchanger below the cab window used in snowshed territory on Donner, where the electric staff system was used to authorize train movements. *Courtesy Munson Paddock Collection, Railroad Museum of Pennsylvania (PHMC)*

the century by the North Pacific Coast, a narrow gauge line serving the Bay Area and familiar to SP managers.

SP worked with Baldwin in reversing the Mallet configuration: the smokebox faced the tender, while the firebox rode at the front of the boiler, and a distinctively designed cab was at the head of the locomotive. To alleviate safety concerns of the crews, heavy protective plates were installed at the front of the cab. Key to enabling the unusual orientation of SP's cab-forward Mallets was SP's choice of fuel. Because the trains were oil burners, it was relatively simple to deliver fuel to the firebox with the tenders at the far end of the locomotives. If the trains had been coal burners, such an arrangement would have been impractical.

In 1911, SP returned to Baldwin with an order for 12 2-6-6-2 cab-forward Mallets for passenger service: the MM-2 (Mallet Mogul). Although the two-wheel leading pony truck proved troublesome and was ultimately replaced with a four-wheel leading truck, the cab-forward concept was successful, and SP continued to order the type from Baldwin. In later years, as compounding fell out of favor, SP converted the early cab-forward types into simple articulateds. In addition, it placed orders for heavy simple articulateds from Baldwin with the cab-forward configuration. The last of these was built in 1944. While none of the original Mallets survive, this final cab-forward was preserved and today is exhibited at the California State Railroad Museum in Sacramento.

MALLETS IN SERVICE

The Mallet type provided extremely high tractive effort because of the number of wheels and high adhesive weight. In addition, other elements of its design contributed to great pulling power. A paper read by Baldwin's Grafton Greenough to the Engineers' Club of Philadelphia on March 21, 1908 (and reprinted in part in Calvin F. Swingle's *Modern American Railway Practice*), explains how a Mallet automatically recovered from wheel-slip when working upgrade:

> . . . in the event of slippage the locomotive immediately recovers itself, for the two engines depend one upon the other for the distribution of the steam. Should the high-pressure engine slip, its exhaust would fill the receiving pipe faster than the low-pressure engine could relieve it, and the resulting back pressure on the high-pressure piston would prevent further slipping. If the low-pressure engine should slip it would exhaust the contents of the receiver until the pressure in the low-pressure cylinders was reduced sufficiently to stop the slipping.
>
> Any continuous slipping can only occur in both engines simultaneously, which can be corrected by the same means that might be necessary for regular types of locomotives under the same circumstances. And these means are usually notching back the throttle to reduce power while applying sand to the rail to increase adhesion.

SPECIFICATIONS
Duluth, Missabe & Northern Class M

Wheel arrangement: 2-8-8-2
High-pressure cylinders: Two 26x32 in.
Low-pressure cylinders: Four 40x32 in.
Drivers: 57 in.
Total engine weight: 436,000 lbs.
Tractive effort: 91,000 lbs.

Ore-hauling Duluth, Missabe & Northern was among the first railroads to take advantage of the 2-8-8-2 Mallet's great pulling power. Baldwin built eight Class M 2-8-8-2s in 1910, followed by four more (Class M-1 and M-2) in 1916 and 1917. They worked for four decades in heavy freight service. *Baldwin image No. 03383, construction No. 35170, courtesy H. L. Broadbelt Baldwin Collection (RR88.2), Railroad Museum of Pennsylvania (PHMC)*

Clemons Logging Company No. 7

Wheel arrangement: 2-6-6-2T

High-pressure cylinders: Two 18x24 in.

Low-pressure cylinders: Two 28x24 in.

Drivers: 44 in.

Total engine weight: 245,500 lbs.

Tractive effort: 42,500 lbs.

By spreading boiler weight over numerous drive wheels, Mallets lowered axle weight while maintaining high tractive effort. After Mallets fell out of favor for heavy road service on most lines, they were built for light-axle-weight applications on slow-speed industrial lines and timber railways. Completed in July 1925, Clemons Logging Company No. 7 was designed for high tractive effort at slow speeds on poor track with tight curves. *Baldwin image No. 9560, construction No. 58529, courtesy H. L. Broadbelt Baldwin Collection (RR88.2), Railroad Museum of Pennsylvania (PHMC)*

The success of the Mallet as a heavy freight hauler made it popular on lines with heavy tonnage. Large numbers of 2-6-6-2s, 2-8-8-0s, and 2-8-8-2s were bought by coal- and ore-hauling lines, and many survived into the early diesel era.

PUSHING THE ENVELOPE

Most Mallets were designed and bought for relatively slow-speed service. The most successful of the type were the ponderous 2-6-6-2s. However, in the early years of Mallet development, several railroads encouraged a variety of unusual and curious applications of the articulated compound. Of these, Baldwin built the most interesting—if not the most successful—examples.

Santa Fe, which had been an ardent supporter of compound locomotives, initially embraced the Mallet type, buying several unusual high-speed 2-6-6-2 passenger Mallets from Baldwin in 1910–1911. The most bizarre of these were experimental types with flexible boilers. The company also experimented with some curious wheel arrangements, including the 4-4-6-2, in an effort to achieve greater performance.

SPECIFICATIONS
Santa Fe No. 1170

Wheel arrangement: 2-6-6-2
High-pressure cylinders: Two 24x28 in.
Low-pressure cylinders: Two 38x28 in.
Drivers: 69 in.
Total engine weight: 392,300 lbs.
Tractive effort: n/a

The Mallets' ability to negotiate curves was intrinsic to their success. Especially unusual were Santa Fe's flexible-boiler locomotives of 1910. Santa Fe 2-6-6-2 No. 1170 demonstrates its flexibility on a curve, presumably near Baldwin's plant. *Construction No. 34862, courtesy H. L. Broadbelt Baldwin Collection (RR88.2), Railroad Museum of Pennsylvania (PHMC)*

Baldwin worked with Santa Fe to develop two different arrangements of flexible boilers in an effort to improve vertical and lateral flexibility when negotiating curves. In both, the forward engine was rigidly attached to the boiler segment it carried. The boiler portion above the forward engine served as a type of feedwater heater. For the flexible boiler, Santa Fe tried both a double ball-and-socket connection joint and an accordion joint using riveted steel rings. The March 1911 issue of *Railway and*

Santa Fe 2-6-6-2 No. 1170 was among first of several Mallets constructed with a highly unusual flexible boiler with ball-in-socket connections. Even stranger were similar locomotives that used an accordion connection. Santa Fe's flexible-boiler design was an ill-founded attempt to make very powerful passenger locomotives. *Baldwin builder's card, Railroad Museum of Pennsylvania (PHMC)*

Locomotive Engineering described the ball-and-socket connection: ". . . the connection consists of two cast iron sleeves, fitted one within the other and proved with snap rings to keep the joint tight. Each sleeve forms a ball joint with a cast iron ring, which is bolted to the shell of the corresponding boiler section."

The accordion joint consisted of 60 rings made from high-carbon steel. These were as thick as No. 14 wire, 10 inches wide, and 75½ inches in diameter. *Railway and Locomotive Engineering* described this arrangement as "made with a set, so that, when placed adjacent to each other, they form a series of V-shaped joints. The adjacent rings are riveted together at the inside and bolted at the outside and the connection is bolted in place between the front and rear boiler sections."

As with a great many experimental locomotives, Santa Fe's flexible-boiler Mallets proved more of a problem than they were worth. Within a few years of construction all of its flexible-boiler locomotives were separated and rebuilt as conventional, non-articulated simple engines.

In 1911, Santa Fe pursued the Mallet design in another direction with assembly of 10 2-10-10-2 types in its shops using parts from existing 2-10-2s and new driving gear and boiler sections provided by Baldwin. Not surprisingly, these engines also proved failures and were later rebuilt into conventional 2-10-2s. If these avenues were not sufficiently outlandish, Santa Fe seriously contemplated even more bizarre locomotives and requested that Baldwin draft plans for a freakish cab-forward 2-8-8-8-8-2 "Quadruplex" and a

SPECIFICATIONS

Erie Railroad No. 5014

Wheel arrangement: 2-8-8-8-2
High-pressure cylinders: Two 36x32 in.
Low-pressure cylinders: Four 36x32 in.
Drivers: 69 in.
Total engine weight: 853,050 lbs.
Tractive effort: 160,000 lbs.

Erie's three 2-8-8-8-2s were among the more curious of Baldwin's large locomotives. Most famous of the batch was No. 5014, named *Matt H. Shay*, originally numbered 2603. Built in 1914, the Triplex locomotives were so large they couldn't be shopped at Erie's works at Susquehanna, Pennsylvania, where they were based. When heavy work was required, they were sent to Lehigh Valley's shops at Sayre, Pennsylvania. *Construction No. 41308, courtesy H. L. Broadbelt Baldwin Collection (RR88.2), Railroad Museum of Pennsylvania (PHMC)*

2-8-8-8-8-8-2 "Quintuplex." The aim was to put as much power behind one throttle as possible. Strange as it may seem, the essential concept was valid. A generation later, Santa Fe was the first to order a large fleet of diesel-electric locomotives that accomplished this goal using more practical technology.

TRIPLEX

The Erie Railroad and later the Virginian Railway both experimented with Mallet types with *three* complete sets of cylinders and running gear called Triplexes. Although these were deemed technological failures, they were among the largest and most interesting applications of the Mallet concept.

Erie had ordered three massive 0-8-8-0s from Baldwin's competitor Alco in 1906 for use as pushers over Gulf Summit (east of Susquehanna, Pennsylvania). In 1914, Erie looked to Baldwin to push the concept of enormous helper locomotives a step further and ordered three massive 2-8-8-8-2s. Each locomotive featured three pairs of 36x32-inch cylinders, two sets of which rode below the boiler and a third below the tender. All the cylinders were the same size, but those powering the middle engine worked on high-pressure steam directly from the boiler; the right cylinder exhausted into the front engine, and the left cylinder exhausted into the rear engine. Thus, the triplex was a variation of the double-expansion engine and not a triple-expansion engine. The locomotive weighed 853,050 pounds with 63-inch driving wheels. The boiler operated at 210 psi, and, in theory, the locomotive could produce 160,000 pounds starting tractive effort, which gave Erie's 2-8-8-8-2s the title of the most powerful locomotives in the world. But the triplex did not live up to its billing. The machines suffered from poor performance and difficult maintenance as a result of their complex equipment and design flaws. As with many early efforts at producing very powerful locomotives, the boiler failed to produce enough steam to power the engines for any length of time. Also, in service, engineers found it extremely difficult to balance the power of the triplex's three engines. Among the problems, as the fuel and water were exhausted, the weight on the tender dropped, causing the rear set of drivers to lose adhesion and slip. Another chronic problem was that the rear cylinders exhausted through a stack on the tender that did not add to firebox draft. Losing 50 percent of the draft, the fire didn't receive enough air to produce adequate combustion for the amount of steam needed. As the engine worked harder, it tended to suffocate itself. Although the design theory assumed that the locomotives would not require sustained power, since they were only to work as rear-end helpers for about 11 miles, in practice they tended to run out of steam before reaching Gulf Summit.

Appalachian coal hauler Virginian had been a significant proponent of enormous Mallet compounds that allowed it to haul some of the heaviest trains in the world, from West Virginia mines to docks at Sewalls Point, Virginia. Although the Erie triplex failed to perform adequately, Virginian was curious about the potential of the type and in 1916 ordered from Baldwin a single, slightly modified triplex with a 2-8-8-8-4 wheel arrangement. While not as massive as the Erie machines, Virginian's locomotive, classed XA,

suffered from the same basic design flaws and was deemed even less successful. None of the triplexes remained in service long, and all were ultimately rebuilt into less complicated locomotives.

BALDWIN'S 50,000TH LOCOMOTIVE

Keenly aware of the significance placed on milestone locomotives, Baldwin established the practice of reserving production numbers ending in "000" for special prototypes, experimentals, and other noteworthy locomotives produced at its works. While decades had passed before the company completed its first 1,000 locomotives, by the late nineteenth century it was churning out engines at rates often exceeding 2,000 locomotives a year.

Locomotive 5000, a novel 4-2-2 type designed for fast passenger service on the Philadelphia & Reading (see page 22), was completed in April 1880. Completed in June 1889 for Northern Pacific, Baldwin No. 10000 was part of a group of the heaviest class of Consolidations on record at that time. No. 20000 was a 4-6-0 experimental Vauclain-designed Balanced compound finished in February 1902. Locomotive No. 30000 was Pennsylvania Railroad K3s Pacific 8661, completed at Eddystone in June 1913. The next milestone was locomotive 40000 and Southern Railway No. 4009, finished in September 1918 and part of an order for 12 large 2-8-8-2 Mallet compounds.

Like many of Baldwin's most distinctive or noteworthy locomotives, No. 50000, a Southern Railway Ls-1 Mallet (the full railroad designation is too complex to reprint here), was given a special write-up and was the subject of a Baldwin brochure entitled, appropriately, *The Fifty Thousandth Locomotive*. Interestingly, Baldwin's competitor Alco produced its 50,000th locomotive in 1911, an experimental large-boiler Pacific used to show off the capabilities of the type. This became the primary influence for Pennsylvania's famous K4s class Pacific that would come to dwarf the relevance of its K3s Pacific built by Baldwin.

Southern's Ls-1 Mallets were designed specifically for service between Appalachia and Bristol, Virginia, on an unusually tortuous and steeply graded line. Here, for 8 miles between

6932

mileposts 57 and 65, the line featured 10-degree curves and an average grade of 1.7 percent, with a maximum gradient of 3.4 percent. This put it among the steepest main lines in the eastern United States. The railroad's principal commodity on this route was coal moved in heavy trains.

As with most varieties of compounds, Baldwin's 50,000th locomotive had special valve arrangements to allow high-pressure steam to be admitted to all cylinders as an aid in starting. In this case, the "Simplex" compound system was employed. *The Fifty Thousandth Locomotive*, which details many aspects of the locomotive, explains as follows:

In order to operate the locomotive in single expansion, as in starting, or when there is danger of stalling, live steam is admitted against the intercepting valve piston through a manually controlled valve in the cab. The intercepting and reducing valves then take such a position that the high-pressure exhaust is discharged up the stack, while live steam is admitted at reduced pressure direct to the receiver pipe.

When the valve in the cab was closed, the locomotive automatically reverted to compound operation.

SPECIFICATIONS

Baldwin No. 60000

Wheel arrangement: 4-10-2

High-pressure cylinder: One 27x32 in.

Low-pressure cylinders: Two 27x32 in.

Drivers: 63½ in.

Total engine weight: 457,500 lbs.

Tractive effort: 82,500 lbs.

Locomotive No. 60000, so numbered because it was the 60,000th locomotive built by Baldwin, was never sold or replicated. The original machine was donated to Philadelphia's Franklin Institute, where it remains as an integral display. It's ironic that one of Baldwin's most perfectly preserved locomotives is this highly unusual experimental rather than one of the thousands of ordinary engines that hauled freight and passenger trains across North America. *Baldwin image No. 9772, construction No. 60000, courtesy H. L. Broadbelt Baldwin Collection (RR88.2), Railroad Museum of Pennsylvania (PHMC)*

locomotive and the results of tests conducted at Pennsylvania Railroad's famed Altoona test plant in a brochure entitled *Locomotive Number 60000—An Experimental Locomotive*, authored in part by Paul T. Warner and Lawford H. Fry. In this, Warner explains the design concept behind No. 60000:

> *Up to a certain period, development of locomotive design brought with it mainly an increase in weight of individual locomotives, the increase in power being proportionate to the increase in weight. This increase in power made possible notable economies in railroading. Of late years, however, the demand for still further economies has led locomotive designers to strive to increase the efficiency of the locomotive, and thus give increased power per unit of locomotive weight. Among the means adopted successfully to this end are the use of superheated steam, various fuel and labor-saving devices, improved boiler design, more efficient steam distribution, and refinements in design and materials for locomotive parts.*

In the 1920s, Alco had developed three-cylinder simple locomotives for commercial applications, yet three-cylinder compounds, which had been in use in a number of European countries, remained unusual in the United States. On No. 60000, the central high-pressure cylinder received steam directly from the superheater using a single steam pipe. It exhausted into the pair of outside cylinders. While the central cylinder powered the second pair of driving wheels via a cranked axle, the outside cylinders powered the third set of drives using outside rods in the conventional fashion.

The locomotive is understood to have performed very well. While elements of its design contributed to the body of steam locomotive knowledge, the machine contained too many unusual features to warrant mass production. It was ultimately donated to Philadelphia's Franklin Institute where it remains today as a star exhibit and one of few surviving examples of compound locomotive design in America.

Ultimately, Southern ordered 23 of these Baldwin compound 2-8-8-2s, the last delivered in 1926. By that time, compounding had largely fallen out of favor, so Southern ordered another eight 2-8-8-2s of a simple-articulated design (high pressure to all cylinders.)

BALDWIN 60000

Baldwin made its final foray into compounding in 1926, when it designed and constructed a very unusual experimental three-cylinder 4-10-2, symbolically assigned construction number 60000. This was a test bed for several different concepts aimed at improving the overall thermal efficiency of steam locomotive design. Among its most distinctive features were a water-tube firebox, a relatively high operating pressure of 350 psi, and a three-cylinder compound arrangement. Baldwin published a detailed description of this

Reading Iron Company, an affiliate of the Philadelphia & Reading Railroad, ordered this compact camelback 0-4-0 switcher that was essentially constructed to P&R specifications and carried the P&R A5-A classification. It was completed in January 1906 and photographed in February of that year. Like many P&R anthracite burners, it featured a Wootten firebox. *Baldwin image No. 02111, construction No. 29304, courtesy H. L. Broadbelt Baldwin Collection (RR88.2), Railroad Museum of Pennsylvania (PHMC)*

CHAPTER THREE

20TH CENTURY STEAM LOCOMOTIVES

Opposite: This comparison view exposed on February 21, 1941, shows the size difference between a Western Maryland 4-6-6-4 Challenger built for heavy road-freight service and a 2-6-6-2 designed for low-axle-weight industrial applications. *Baldwin image No. 12005-2, courtesy H. L. Broadbelt Baldwin Collection (RR88.2), Railroad Museum of Pennsylvania (PHMC)*

RAPID EXPANSION OF THE American railroad network during the last half of the nineteenth century stimulated a dramatic increase in the demand for locomotives. As the railroad industry gained momentum, significant advancements in infrastructure—stronger bridges, improved rights-of-way, and more robust track structure—enabled railroads to increase the maximum axle weight and thus operate heavier locomotives. Other developments, including the automatic air brake, improved couplers and drawbars, and automatic block signals, allowed for safe operation of substantially longer, faster, and heavier trains. As a result, the size and output of average road locomotives (as compared with switchers or specialized locomotives) increased rapidly.

In 1840 a heavy 4-4-0 weighed 26,000 pounds, while in 1880 a typical heavy passenger-service 4-4-0 weighed 70,000 pounds and placed 46,000 pounds on driving wheels (thus a 23-ton axle weight). A typical freight-service 2-8-0 weighed just over 100,000 pounds with 88,000 pounds on drivers, which worked out to 22,000 pounds axle weight. By 1900, the weight of a 4-4-0 in fast passenger service had nearly doubled to 135,000 pounds, while 2-8-0s frequently weighed more than 200,000 pounds.

By the 1890s, builders were seeking means of further increasing locomotive power and speed while striving to achieve greater thermal efficiency. Through the nineteenth century, locomotive

12005-2
2-21-41

Nevada-California-Oregon Railway was a three-foot-gauge line operating north from Reno, Nevada, to Alturas, California, and beyond to Lakeview, Oregon. Baldwin built this handsome 4-6-0 for the line in 1911 and photographed it inside the plant. Much of the N-C-O was later integrated into parts of the Southern Pacific and Western Pacific standard gauge networks, while N-C-O No. 11 was sold to Hawaii's Oahu Railway. *Baldwin image No. 3773, construction No. 37325, courtesy H. L. Broadbelt Baldwin Collection (RR88.2), Railroad Museum of Pennsylvania (PHMC)*

size had been limited by the capacity of the firebox and boiler. While some large experimental locomotives had been built, these typically suffered from inadequate firebox and boiler capacity, resulting in heavy engines that ran out of steam too quickly for most practical applications. Such monsters were often assigned as helper locomotives where high power and tractive effort were required at slow speed for short stretches.

Baldwin's engineering innovations in the last years of the nineteenth century overcame firebox limitations and ultimately evolved into new standard types. Change was relatively slow and tended to follow an evolutionary process over successive designs.

In 1893, Baldwin built a novel Vauclain compound for demonstration at the Columbian Exposition in Chicago to show off the potential of a new wheel arrangement. This elegantly decorated machine was appropriately named *Columbia*. Its 2-4-2 arrangement defined what became known as the Columbia type, featuring abnormally tall drivers (84 ½ inches in diameter), a leading pony truck (also with unusually large wheels),

and most significantly a trailing truck beneath the firebox. This last feature proved to be the type's most lasting development.

While *Columbia* was not the first locomotive to employ pony wheels below the firebox, its application of this design set a precedent advanced by Baldwin on later locomotive types. Trailing pony wheels provided added support at the back of the engine, increasing stability and providing a better ride. More importantly, the pony wheels supported a portion of the firebox, enabling construction of a deeper firebox, in turn significantly increasing steam-generating capacity. Baldwin elaborated on this concept in its 1912 publication, *Recent Development of the Locomotive*:

> *With the desire for additional heating surface requisite for maintaining higher speeds, it was found that advantage could be taken of the trailing truck to bring the firebox entirely back of the drivers and thereby make it deeper, as the truck*

wheel was so much lower than the drivers. This gave longer tubes and a better firebox for the proper combustion of fuel, and the increase in firebox volume and heating surface has been considered so essential.

With *Columbia*, the firebox remained within the locomotive's width between the wheels, but with a later adaptation of the 2-4-2 arrangement Baldwin took the next step. In 1895, Baldwin built for Chicago, Burlington & Quincy a 2-4-2 type with a wide-grate firebox supported by the trailing truck. The firebox

SPECIFICATIONS
Long Island Rail Road No. 1
Wheel arrangement: 4-4-2
Cylinders: Two 19½x26 in.
Drivers: 76 in.
Total engine weight: 173,600 lbs.
Tractive effort: 23,675 lbs.

Long Island Rail Road No. 1 was one of two such 4-4-2 camelbacks Baldwin completed for the line in April 1901. The divided-cab arrangement, while common during the period on the anthracite roads, was unusual on LIRR. The locomotive was retired in 1929. *Baldwin image No. 1458, construction No. 18937, courtesy H. L. Broadbelt Baldwin Collection (RR88.2), Railroad Museum of Pennsylvania (PHMC)*

SPECIFICATIONS
Norfolk & Western No. 450

Wheel arrangement: 4-8-0

Cylinders: Two 21x30 in.

Drivers: 56 in.

Total engine weight: n/a

Tractive effort: n/a

Compared with the ubiquitous 2-8-0 Consolidations, the 4-8-0 Twelve-Wheeler was relatively rare. Norfolk & Western was partial to the 4-8-0 and had one of the largest rosters of them in the United States. N&W 4-8-0 No. 450 was built in April 1906. The similar N&W 475 survives today on Pennsylvania's Strasburg Rail Road as an excursion engine. *Baldwin image No. 02161, construction No. 27958, courtesy H. L. Broadbelt Baldwin Collection (RR88.2), Railroad Museum of Pennsylvania (PHMC)*

was no longer limited by the width of the locomotive between the wheels. This locomotive, like others of the 2-4-2 arrangement, suffered from poor tracking and so remained an obscure application, yet its wide firebox with rear supporting truck was soon incorporated into another new design, the 4-4-2.

ATLANTICS

Baldwin built the first 4-4-2 type in 1895 for Atlantic Coast Line; the arrangement, so named for its first operator, has become universally known as the Atlantic type. Although this wheel arrangement would seem an obvious expansion of the successful 4-4-0 type with the trailing truck adopted from the experimental 2-4-2, in fact, the earliest 4-4-2 was a variation of the 4-6-0, with the rear pair of drivers converted to trailing wheels (with significantly lower axles) to allow for the larger firebox.

Initially the 4-4-2 type was built in relatively small numbers and continued to employ conservatively sized fireboxes. Within a few years the type came into its own and was developed by various builders with a wide firebox and tall drivers as a fast express passenger locomotive. A high-capacity boiler with high operating pressure allowed construction of some very impressive 4-4-2s

that produced high horsepower and high speeds. The 4-4-2's success resulted in large numbers built by Baldwin and other manufacturers over the next 12 years

MIKADOS

The advantage of the trailing truck resulted in a host of new types. The successful 2-8-0 heavy-freight hauler was adapted into the 2-8-2, which ultimately emerged as the most popular steam freight design in twentieth-century America. On the 2-8-2, the trailing truck was initially used to support a firebox designed to burn inferior fuel. In 1897, Baldwin received an order from Japan for the type. As a result, the 2-8-2 became known as the Mikado type for the popular Gilbert and Sullivan comic opera *The Mikado*, which was set in Japan.

Among the first domestic 2-8-2 applications was Baldwin's adaptation of the type for narrow gauge service on the Denver & Rio Grande. Over the next few years, 2-8-2s built by Baldwin and its new competitor, Alco, achieved limited acceptance as a standard gauge freight hauler; it wasn't until after 1910 that the Mikado enjoyed universal application for mainline work. After 1914, orders for 2-8-2s outpaced those for the more traditional

2-8-0, and the 2-8-2 enjoyed status as the standard heavy-freight locomotive on many railroads until the end of the steam era.

Indeed, the 2-8-2's ample firebox and boiler, combined with four pairs of drivers and a well-balanced design, made the Mikado ideal for most mainline freight services. The locomotive was capable of sustained speed and had excellent pulling and tracking capabilities. Its wheel arrangement was also adapted for logging lines, where both light axle weight and high tractive effort were operational requirements. Another advantage of the 2-8-2 was its ability to make reverse moves at higher speeds than 2-8-0s, a valuable trait on sinuous lines with numerous reverse curves.

SPECIFICATIONS
Lehigh & Hudson River No. 23
Wheel arrangement: 4-6-0
Cylinders: Two 21x26 in.
Drivers: 64 in.
Total engine weight: n/a
Tractive effort: n/a

Lehigh & Hudson River was one of several anthracite region railways that operated camelback 4-6-0s. Locomotive No. 23 was completed in February 1907 and photographed on March 6 that year. *Baldwin image No. 2325, construction No. 30268, courtesy H. L. Broadbelt Baldwin Collection (RR88.2), Railroad Museum of Pennsylvania (PHMC)*

SPECIFICATIONS
Lehigh Valley No. 681

Wheel arrangement: 4-4-2

Cylinders: Two 20x26 in.

Drivers: 76½ in.

Total engine weight: 187,200 lbs.

Tractive effort: n/a

Completed in July 1903, Lehigh Valley
4-4-2 Atlantic No. 681 was typical of the
railroad's express passenger locomotives
of the period. Among other named trains,
it was assigned to the Lehigh's famed,
fast-running *Black Diamond Express*.
*Baldwin image No. 1732, construction
No. 22476, courtesy H. L. Broadbelt
Baldwin Collection (RR88.2), Railroad
Museum of Pennsylvania (PHMC)*

PRAIRIES, PACIFICS, AND MOUNTAINS

Early in the twentieth century, the successful 2-6-0 was expanded into the 2-6-2 Prairie type, a locomotive embraced by Midwestern lines looking for fast engines for freight and passenger services. Stability problems soon relegated this type to more conservative designs largely for branch-line services.

The development of the 4-6-2 as a heavy passenger-service locomotive was among the significant milestones in early twentieth-century locomotive development. Although this wheel arrangement had been tried several times in the late nineteenth century, it wasn't until 1902, when Alco's Brooks Works built an order of 4-6-2s for the Missouri Pacific with a wide firebox supported by a radial trailing truck, that the 4-6-2 was established as a modern type. Designed for heavy mainline passenger services, it was named the Pacific type, acknowledging the MoPac's pioneer application. It was a logical expansion of the 4-6-0 and 4-4-2 types, while overcoming the stability problems associated with the 2-6-2 Prairies when worked at speed. The Pacific's large boiler allowed for sustained speed, and its six-coupled drivers and four-wheel leading truck gave it a good ride with good traction, an ideal combination for the demands of American passenger services. Keys to its success over four-coupled types were the rapid increase in the weight of passenger trains and the desire for greater train speeds. Passenger trains

SPECIFICATIONS
East Broad Top No. 12
Wheel arrangement: 2-8-2 three-foot-gauge
Cylinders: Two 17x24 in.
Drivers: 48 in.
Total engine weight: 117,800 lbs.
Tractive effort: 19,600 lbs.

Since its beginnings in the early 1870s, Pennsylvania three-foot-gauge East Broad Top bought its locomotives from Baldwin. The line was unusual among American narrow gauge railroads not only because it maintained its common-carrier slim gauge well into the twentieth century but because it ordered substantially heavier motive power, making it among just a few domestic railroads to order relatively large narrow gauge steam locomotives. No. 12, built in December 1911, was the first of its Mikados. The locomotive has been preserved and remained on the EBT in 2009. *Baldwin image No. 3763, construction No. 37325, courtesy H. L. Broadbelt Baldwin Collection (RR88.2), Railroad Museum of Pennsylvania (PHMC)*

had grown longer and heavier as a result of rising ridership. Train consists were more likely to include dining cars and "head-end" traffic. Furthermore, car weights increased by a third or more as a result of the switch to all-steel construction during the first two decades of the century.

Rapidly accepted as the new standard mainline passenger locomotive, the Pacific displaced the Atlantic and American types and remained America's preferred passenger locomotive until mass-produced diesel-electric road diesels supplanted it in the 1940s. Although generally thought of as a passenger design,

SPECIFICATIONS
Saginaw Timber Company No. 2

Wheel arrangement: 2-8-2

Cylinders: Two 18x24 in.

Drivers: 44 in.

Total engine weight: 141,150 lbs.

Tractive effort: 27,000 lbs.

Built for Michigan's Saginaw Timber Company, this Mikado was photographed at Baldwin's plant two days before Christmas 1912. Today it is preserved on the Mid-Continent Railway at North Freedom, Wisconsin, where it served as an excursion engine in the 1990s. *Baldwin image No. 4230, construction No. 38967, courtesy H. L. Broadbelt Baldwin Collection (RR88.2), Railroad Museum of Pennsylvania (PHMC)*

SPECIFICATIONS
Pennsylvania Railroad L1s*

Wheel arrangement: 2-8-2

Cylinders: Two 27x30 in.

Drivers: 62 in.

Total engine weight: 320,700 lbs.

Tractive effort: 57,850 lbs.

* From *Railroad Mechanical Engineer*

Pennsylvania Railroad L1s Mikado No. 9722 was photographed on March 21, 1917, and featured in an article in the June 1917 *Railroad Mechanical Engineer*. Significant to the L1s design was that it shared major component specifications with the railroad's successful K4s Pacific. In fact, the L1s and K4s boilers were interchangeable. At PRR's Altoona test plant the L1s 2-8-2 demonstrated 25 percent higher tractive effort than the H-9s 2-8-0. *Baldwin image No. 6354, courtesy H. L. Broadbelt Baldwin Collection (RR88.2), Railroad Museum of Pennsylvania (PHMC)*

SPECIFICATIONS

New Haven Railroad No. 1093

Wheel arrangement: 4-6-2

Cylinders: Two 24x28 in.

Drivers: 79 in.

Total engine weight: n/a

Tractive effort: n/a

This is a relatively unusual view of a new New Haven Railroad Pacific type at Baldwin's Eddystone plant in January 1913. The photograph is interesting, not just for the nonstandard three-quarter angle and the lack of opaquing, but because the engine is backlit. *Baldwin image No. 4285, construction No. 39175, courtesy H. L. Broadbelt Baldwin Collection (RR88.2), Railroad Museum of Pennsylvania (PHMC)*

Brand-new Pennsylvania Railroad M1a Mountain type No. 6707 basks in the morning sun at Eddystone in April 1930. Of the 100 examples of this type built, this was one of 50 produced by Baldwin and was considered among the ultimate developments of the 4-8-2. PRR designed them for freight and passenger service on its busy Middle Division between Harrisburg and Altoona. Among the characteristics of the M1a design that distinguished it from the earlier M1 were one-piece cast-steel cylinders with inside steam-delivery pipes. *Baldwin image No. 10569, construction No. 61295, courtesy H. L. Broadbelt Baldwin Collection (RR88.2), Railroad Museum of Pennsylvania (PHMC)*

in certain instances the Pacific was built as a fast freight locomotive as well.

In 1911, Chesapeake & Ohio worked with Alco to design a new heavy passenger locomotive that blended characteristics of the 2-8-2 Mikado with those of the heavy 4-6-2 Pacific, using the previously untried 4-8-2 wheel arrangement. High adhesion and a large boiler made for an outstanding locomotive in graded territory. Although first built by Alco, over the next 20 years the 4-8-2 type developed through several builders as both a heavy passenger and heavy road-freight locomotive known as

the Mountain type. One of the most magnificent applications of the type was Pennsylvania Railroad's M1 class, many built by Baldwin in the 1920s. It was further refined by PRR as the M1a, a class built by Baldwin, Lima, and Altoona in 1930.

PARADIGM SHIFTS

Baldwin's business had blossomed in the final years of the nineteenth century, and during the first years of the twentieth century, the company reached the zenith of its production and influence. In his book *Baldwin Locomotive Works 1831–1915*,

John K. Brown notes a high-water mark in the company's production in 1906 when Baldwin's Broad Street factory employed more than 17,400 men and turned out 2,666 locomotives. By comparison, it took Baldwin 37 years (1832 to 1869) to construct its first 2,000 locomotives. The next 2,000 were built in just 7 years. During 1906, the works completed its 28,000th machine. Although no one knew it then, Baldwin was at the height of its business.

Broad Street had been the mainstay of its locomotive production since old Matthias Baldwin himself established the factory in 1835. Although expanded many times, by the early twentieth century the site was no longer suited to the company's production volume or modern locomotive sizes. Baldwin was facing increasing competition from Alco—formed in 1901 from several of Baldwin's competitors, including Schenectady and Brooks—and required more space. In addition, refinement of its manufacturing process was crucial to Baldwin's building larger and more powerful locomotives.

In 1906, under the direction of Samuel Vauclain, the company began construction of a new locomotive plant at Eddystone, Pennsylvania, south of Philadelphia and near the B&O and Pennsy main lines toward Baltimore and Washington. Over the next two decades it gradually transferred production to this much larger facility. Despite a forward-looking management and big plans for the future, Baldwin would face an increasingly difficult path.

But future changes were more profound than Baldwin management could have anticipated in 1906. Brown categorizes the complex factors that influenced Baldwin's business, while tracing the company's decline over the coming years. The Hepburn Act of 1906 was a fulcrum point in the industry, giving the Interstate Commerce Commission greater powers to regulate the steam railroads. Although not immediately evident, this act changed the ability of American railroads to compete effectively for traffic, thus constraining profits, limiting the industry's ability to invest, and contributing to the loss of railroad transport supremacy.

Although the industry had its peaks and valleys, up until this time railroad business had been growing at a phenomenal rate, with companies constructing new lines and experiencing significant annual increases in both freight and passenger traffic. The Hepburn Act didn't immediately strangle the industry; change was slow, and it came in variety of guises. Yet, within a decade, railroad market growth had stalled, and railroads lost the incentive and ability to generate sufficient capital for large-scale improvements to their physical plants. Their route structures stopped growing, and the business began to stagnate.

Other changes contributed to significant and broad-reaching effects on transport, and thus railroad demand for new locomotives. Especially important was the emergence and growth of petroleum-fueled highway transport. During the early twentieth century, highways had negligible effects on railroad traffic, but gradually over the next six decades a combination of increased railroad regulation, improved motor transport technology, government-subsidized road-building, and a dramatic rise in labor costs resulted in a fundamental shift in intercity transport.

These changes forced Baldwin and the other locomotive manufacturers to produce more efficient locomotives. However, development of more powerful and more efficient locomotives within a stagnant and later declining market meant sales of far fewer locomotives. Considering the domestic market, Bruce points to 1905 as the peak year for locomotive orders (for all commercial builders). That year, railroads ordered approximately 6,300 new machines. Over the next three decades the average numbers of locomotives ordered from all builders would slide precipitously, while the power from the average machine would grow enormously. Baldwin's business reflected more than just domestic sales, and exports helped offset domestic declines for a few years. Notably, the demand for locomotives during the two world wars made for a spike in Baldwin production. Nevertheless, the Great Depression saw production plummet to nearly zero for a few years. Except during World War II, the builder never again enjoyed sales even approaching the robust volumes it had reached in the early years of the twentieth century.

SPECIFICATIONS
Belt Railway of Chicago No. 72
Wheel arrangement: 0-6-0
Cylinders: Two 20x26 in.
Drivers: 51 in.
Total engine weight: n/a
Tractive effort: n/a

Opposite: Although originally built for Chicago & Western Indiana in November 1905, this 0-6-0 switcher was sold to Belt Railroad of Chicago. The utilitarian requirements of switching locomotives rarely caught the attention of the trade press. Today, a large number of switchers survive at museums and on tourist railways and thus remain familiar to observers. *Baldwin image No. 02078, construction No. 29764, courtesy H. L. Broadbelt Baldwin Collection (RR88.2), Railroad Museum of Pennsylvania (PHMC)*

SPECIFICATIONS

Pacific Portland Cement No. 2

Wheel arrangement: 0-4-0T

Cylinders: Two 15x24 in.

Drivers: 44 in.

Total engine weight: n/a

Tractive effort: n/a

Switchers were part of the fabric of industrial America in the early twentieth century. Industrial switchers like Pacific Portland Cement No. 2, built in October 1904, were constructed alongside large road locomotives. In the small-switcher business, Baldwin competed with a number of firms, such as Porter and Davenport, that specialized in small steam locomotives. This image is unusual among the Baldwin locomotive photos because it has not been opaqued and shows the Baldwin roundhouse, where many of the builder's photos were exposed. In the background is a New Haven tender. *Baldwin image No. 1934, construction No. 24782, courtesy H. L. Broadbelt Baldwin Collection (RR88.2), Railroad Museum of Pennsylvania (PHMC)*

SEEKING GREATER EFFICIENCY

While locomotive proportions grew and new types were developed to meet the economic challenges of the industry, many of the most important changes involved technological improvements and new appliances inside the engines. While external changes, such as the development of new wheel arrangements and the application of streamlined shrouding, are easily appreciated by casual study, the most important changes were more subtle. The advent of new devices, application of new and improved materials, and improved methods of design and construction were largely invisible to the casual observer.

Especially important to advancing locomotive design were developments in cast-steel technology. Steel offered significantly greater strength than iron and allowed the construction of boilers with much greater strength and thus higher operating pressure. Cast steel allowed for significant weight reduction of

other key components. Baldwin's *Recent Development of the Locomotive* relates:

> *In the replacement of [iron] forgings, cast steel has also rendered an important service; the most notable example of this is in locomotive frames. For years these were made of iron worked under the steam hammer, and, as frames were of large sections, it was very difficult to properly weld the pedestals and braces together. When the sections were not over four inches in thickness there was little difficulty, but even then it was found that the welds, in spite of the best care, had often been imperfectly formed and would in service pull apart. With five-inch frames, which are now [1912] common, and six-inch frames, which are*

SPECIFICATIONS
Long Island Rail Road No. 22

Wheel arrangement: 2-6-2T

Cylinders: Two 18x26 in.

Drivers: 63 in.

Total engine weight: n/a

Tractive effort: n/a

Baldwin completed this suburban tank locomotive in March 1904 for Long Island Rail Road. It was later resold to Central Railroad of New Jersey. Bidirectional tank engines were well suited to suburban passenger services because they didn't require turning facilities at the end of the run. While tank locomotives were common on British railways, the concept was unusual in America. *Baldwin image No. 1860, construction No. 24008, courtesy H. L. Broadbelt Baldwin Collection (RR88.2), Railroad Museum of Pennsylvania (PHMC)*

SPECIFICATIONS
Baldwin Geared Demonstrator

Wheel arrangement: B-B

Cylinders: Two 14x16 in.

Drivers: 36 in.

Total engine weight: 142,080 lbs.

Tractive effort: n/a

The three best-known geared logging locomotives were the Climax, Heisler, and Lima Shay types. Baldwin made an effort to secure a portion of this business and developed its own geared locomotive intended for logging and industrial service on steeply graded and uneven track. This geared truck demonstrator was photographed at the Eddystone shops in November 1912. *Baldwin image No. 4165-2, courtesy H. L. Broadbelt Baldwin Collection (RR88.2), Railroad Museum of Pennsylvania (PHMC)*

SPECIFICATIONS
Charleston Lumber Company No. 3
Wheel arrangement: 2-4-0
Cylinders: Two 9x14 in.
Drivers: 33 in.
Total engine weight: n/a
Tractive effort: n/a

While larger engines were often shipped out coupled in a train, sometimes smaller engines, such as Charleston Lumber Company No. 3, were delivered by flatcar. *Baldwin image No. 2189, construction No. 28398, courtesy H. L. Broadbelt Baldwin Collection (RR88.2), Railroad Museum of Pennsylvania (PHMC)*

being introduced, this work would be very difficult, but cast steel permits the use of a section of almost any size. . . . Many of the more complicated forgings, such as equalizer beams, frame braces, and parts that have been made in the blacksmith shop, are constructed of cast steel, often reducing the weight and at the same time the cost of manufacture.

Cast steel was just one of the many important changes affecting locomotive design and construction. Baldwin's commemorative brochure, *Completion of the Forty-Thousandth Locomotive*, published in 1913, primarily describes the specifications for Pennsylvania Railroad's K3s Pacific (s for "superheated") but also summarizes changes to steam locomotive design over the years, highlighting significant recent advances. It notes increases in boiler weight and capacity by "locomotives used in all classes of service"

while pointing out efficiency improvements made by implementation of the steam superheater and firebrick arch, a deflector made of bricks inside the firebox designed to aid combustion.

The superheater improved the thermal efficiency of the steam locomotive without significant design changes, high implementation expenses, or added maintenance costs. Introduced experimentally in the early years of the twentieth century and widely adopted by 1910, in 1913 the superheater had achieved near universal acceptance as an energy-saving device. Not only were virtually all new locomotives built with superheaters, but many older locomotives were reequipped.

REACHING NEW PLATEAUS

Although 1913 represented a time to reflect on design improvements and remarkable growth in power and efficiency, it was by no means the zenith of locomotive design. Over the next three decades Baldwin and the other major manufacturers, Alco and Lima, refined ever bigger and more efficient locomotives, the largest of which would soon dwarf those then in production.

Rising labor costs encouraged increased locomotive availability and productivity. Historically, locomotives were serviced after every run and only operated over the length of one division—typically about 100 miles. After World War I, a few lines

dramatically increased distances locomotives operated between servicing stops. Railroads also lowered maintenance costs through a variety of small design changes to reduce wear and component stress and thus allow engines more mileage between overhauls.

Refinements included advanced feedwater heaters, metallurgical development, precision counterbalancing, and commercially produced roller bearings. Feedwater heaters further improved thermal efficiency through a reduction in heat loss by employing exhaust gases to heat water before it entered the boiler. Lightweight steel alloys lowered the weight of key components, especially reciprocating parts. Stronger steel produced much lighter rods, drive wheels, and related reciprocating equipment, allowing locomotives to operate safely and efficiently at much higher speeds. This caused less damage to the machinery and eased wear on tracks and infrastructure. Reciprocating forces were further reduced through modern counterbalancing techniques, while roller bearings and improved lubrication allowed for further improvements in efficiency and locomotive availability.

World War I dramatically increased labor costs. Railroading was inherently labor intensive and thus especially susceptible to these changes. While railroads had been implementing

The Baldwin photography collection sometimes documents events rather than specific engines. In May 1922, the West Philadelphia High School girls' class visited Eddystone. Students posed several times for photos. Virginian Railway No. 410 was a unique locomotive rebuilt from the tender engine from the Virginian's ill-fated 2-8-8-8-4 Triplex. *Baldwin image No. 8357A, courtesy H. L. Broadbelt Baldwin Collection (RR88.2), Railroad Museum of Pennsylvania (PHMC)*

SPECIFICATIONS
Baltimore & Ohio No. 5212

Wheel arrangement: 4-6-2

Cylinders: Two 25x28 in.

Drivers: 74 in.

Total engine weight: 288,000 lbs.

Tractive effort: 40,200 lbs.

During World War I, the United States Railroad Administration operated American railroads and established standard locomotive designs in an effort to reduce the variation of types among railroads. Baltimore & Ohio's Class P5 was based on the USRA light Pacific design. Baldwin built the first 20, while the last 10 were Alco products. In 1921, B&O P5 Pacific No. 5212 leads a passenger train on B&O's main line. *Baldwin image No. 8096, courtesy H. L. Broadbelt Baldwin Collection (RR88.2), Railroad Museum of Pennsylvania (PHMC)*

CAPROTTI POPPET VALVE GEAR

ASSEMBLY

REVERSE CRANK

REVERSE ROD

REVERSING SHAFT ARM

TAPPET GUARD

PHOTOGRAPH DEPARTMENT
THE BALDWIN LOCOMOTIVE WORKS
PHILADELPHIA, PA., U. S. A.

In the mid-1920s, Baldwin licensed the Caprotti poppet valve system. A Baldwin advertisement from the period offered a host of advantages: "The Caprotti system gives a 'timed' cut-off with full admission port opening together with an independent exhaust fully open at all cut-offs. . . . Caprotti valve gear economizes fuel, water and lubricating oil." Despite these advantages, the type was only experimentally applied to a few American-built locomotives. *Baldwin image No. 9890-13, courtesy H. L. Broadbelt Baldwin Collection (RR88.2), Railroad Museum of Pennsylvania (PHMC)*

labor-saving devices for decades, after World War I, railroads eagerly sought to improve labor productivity. One solution was to refine ever more reliable and productive locomotives.

Railroads needed to move more goods and passengers using fewer crews and fewer locomotives. By increasing average train speeds, they could better compete with each other and other modes while freeing up track capacity without expensive infrastructure improvements. By the 1920s, emerging intercity highway freight encouraged railroads to increase average freight train speeds to compete more effectively for lucrative small shipments. Also, on the main east–west trunk lines, such as the Pennsylvania Railroad and New York Central, a very high volume of fast passenger trains encouraged railroads to keep freight moving at a faster pace to maintain mainline fluidity. Fast high-power locomotives were designed to fulfill these services. High-drivered Mountain types, bigger Mikados, and powerful Santa Fes emerged in the second decade of the century. Soon, even more powerful types were developed. Other potential solutions were also considered, such as electrification.

OIL BURNERS

The use of oil as a locomotive fuel predates the first commercial diesel locomotives by decades. According to George H. Drury in his *Guide to North American Steam Locomotives*, the first successful application of oil-burning steam locomotives occurred during the 1880s in Russia. Baldwin built an experimental Vauclain compound as an oil burner in 1894, using a Russian system, and tested it on the Baltimore & Ohio and the Reading.

Most eastern lines were blessed with ample supplies of inexpensive coal and had little incentive to seek oil-burning engines. This was not the case in the far West where coal was in short supply. At the end of the nineteenth century, Santa Fe made a pioneering effort to develop oil-burning steam locomotives. Santa Fe had reached Southern California, where oil was plentiful (the state would become the world's leading oil producer in the early years of the twentieth century). Initially, it worked with the Union Oil Company to perfect a device for spraying oil into the firebox. Further firebox adaptation was necessary

This posed and retouched image was featured in the May 1928 *Baldwin Locomotives* magazine with a detailed article on the Western Maryland's steam power. WM Class H-9 2-8-0 No. 805 leads a 100-car coal train in January 1922 on the way from Cumberland to Hagerstown. This was the standard length for loaded trains on the railroad's water-level grade east of Cumberland. WM's H-9s were exceptionally capable and routinely worked roundtrips between Cumberland and Hagerstown in less than 14 hours. *Baldwin image No. 8249, construction No. 54496, courtesy H. L. Broadbelt Baldwin Collection (RR88.2), Railroad Museum of Pennsylvania (PHMC)*

WESTERN MARYLAND RAILWAY
TRAIN OF 100 LOADS
7842 ACTUAL GROSS TONS

to burn oil effectively and efficiently. Oil had to be atomized for proper combustion, and the most effective location of the atomizer required a bit of study. Refining the firewall ensured the necessary draft. Commercial development of oil burners followed a period of intensive experimentation, and by the early twentieth century Santa Fe had successfully adopted oil as its preferred locomotive fuel. Other western lines quickly followed suit—Southern Pacific, Union Pacific, and Western Pacific were among the lines to adopt oil-burning steam locomotives. Baldwin was the leading producer of these machines.

At the 1915 Panama-Pacific International Exposition in San Francisco, Baldwin displayed a variety of modern locomotive types built for western lines. Most were oil burners. Baldwin's brochure for the exhibit explained, "Oil-burning locomotives are proving highly successful, as full steam pressure can be carried under the most severe service conditions; and this fuel is therefore specially suitable for large locomotives in which high powers must be developed for sustained periods."

One advantage of oil-burning engines was a dramatic reduction in residual material following combustion as compared with

SPECIFICATIONS
Milwaukee Road No. 8237

Wheel arrangement: 2-8-2

Cylinders: Two 26x30 in.

Drivers: 63 in.

Total engine weight: n/a

Tractive effort: n/a

In the early 1920s, the Mikado type was the most popular new design for general road freight service. In 1921, Chicago's Kaumann & Fabry Company exposed this 8x10-inch image of Milwaukee Road 2-8-2 No. 8237 with a freight train. The locomotive left Baldwin in November 1920. *Baldwin image No. 7847, construction No. 54000, courtesy H. L. Broadbelt Baldwin Collection (RR88.2), Railroad Museum of Pennsylvania (PHMC)*

SPECIFICATIONS

Southern Pacific No. 3654

Wheel arrangement: 2-10-2

Cylinders: Two 29½x32 in.

Drivers: 63 in.

Total engine weight: 385,900 lbs.

Tractive effort: 75,150 lbs.

Southern Pacific 2-10-2 No. 3654 was one of the locomotives shipped as part of Baldwin's famed *Prosperity Special* in 1921. *Baldwin image No. 7831, construction No. 54314, courtesy H. L. Broadbelt Baldwin Collection (RR88.2), Railroad Museum of Pennsylvania (PHMC)*

coal. This minimized the need to clean cinders and ash from the firebox, which reduced servicing time and costs. Cleaning an oil burner's flues was easily accomplished by throwing an occasional shovelful of sand into the firebox. The forced draft would carry the sand through the flues and up the stack, cleaning the engine of tar and other accumulated fuel waste. Also, fewer sparks were emitted from the stack, an added benefit in areas where the risk of fire was a concern. Finally, in some situations, burning oil was cheaper than burning coal. In 1912, Baldwin estimated that "a dollar's worth of oil would often replace three or four dollars worth of coal."

Not only were oil burners significantly easier to refuel, but they could carry substantially more fuel in the tender, enabling locomotives to travel much longer distances between refueling stops than had been previously possible with coal burners. As

a result, oil burners proved capable of some very long runs. An article in the July 1923 *Baldwin Locomotives* highlights notable long locomotive runs, stating, "Oil is the ideal fuel for exceptionally long runs, as the fire does not have to be cleaned, there are no cinders to accumulate in the front end, and the tubes can be easily cleaned of soot." Among the disadvantages cited for oil-burning engines (though not in this article) was rapid firebox deterioration. In some instances, oil-fired locomotives required firebox renewal two or three times as often as comparable coal burners.

The July 23 article went on to highlight Santa Fe operations, which included seven through locomotive runs greater than 300 miles, mostly handled by oil burners. Between Wellington, Kansas, and Clovis, New Mexico, a distance of 446.3 miles, Santa Fe routinely assigned oil-fired 1309 Pacific-class models (built by Baldwin as balanced compounds in 1911) to passenger trains averaging 10 cars. In general, this line had no more than a 0.6 percent grade (a rise of 6 feet for every 1,000 feet), however there was a short section of 1 percent grade (1 foot rise for every 100 traveled).

Santa Fe continued to extend the lengths of runs made by its fastest passenger locomotives, so by the mid-1930s it routinely ran Baldwin-built 4-6-4 Hudsons from Chicago to La Junta, Colorado. These locomotives had high-capacity tenders that carried up to 7,000 gallons of oil and 20,000 gallons of water. In *The Locomotives That Baldwin Built*, Frederick

Westing describes the publicity run of Santa Fe's Baldwin 4-6-4 No. 3461, which ran the full distance from Chicago to Los Angeles, completing its 2,227.5 mile sprint on December 12, 1937. No. 3461's train varied between 10 and 12 cars, which weighed between 757 and 939 tons. On four occasions—as normally expected—helpers were required on Santa Fe's steepest grades. At times, 3461 reached speeds of up to 90 miles per hour—then Santa Fe's speed limit. Westing wrote that this run was believed to have been the longest completed by a single steam locomotive.

SPECIFICATIONS
Great Northern No. 2100
Wheel arrangement: 2-10-2
Cylinders: Two 31x32 in.
Drivers: 63 in.
Total engine weight: 422,340 lbs.
Tractive effort: 87,100 lbs.

Built in 1923, Great Northern Class Q-1 No. 2100 was an oil burner designed to work heavy freight service on the railroad's transcontinental main line between Whitefish and Cutbank, Montana. In that service, it could haul 75-car trains weighing up to 3,000 tons. *Baldwin image No. 9026, construction No. 57410, courtesy H. L. Broadbelt Baldwin Collection (RR88.2), Railroad Museum of Pennsylvania (PHMC)*

SPECIFICATIONS

Santa Fe No. 3840

Wheel arrangement: 2-10-2

Cylinders: Two 30x32 in.

Drivers: 63 in.

Total engine weight: n/a

Tractive effort: n/a

Santa Fe's 3840 was among the railroad's 3800-class 2-10-2s built between 1919 and 1927. This locomotive was completed in July 1921 and photographed with officials in August 1921. *Baldwin image No. 8040, construction No. 54923, courtesy H. L. Broadbelt Baldwin Collection (RR88.2), Railroad Museum of Pennsylvania (PHMC)*

TEN-COUPLED

Ten-coupled locomotives had been tried since the 1860s. By the early twentieth century a number of railroads were successfully using 2-10-0 Decapods in heavy freight service. In 1902, with the addition of a trailing pony truck, Santa Fe expanded the 2-10-0 into the 2-10-2 Santa Fe type, initially to aid when reversing these large locomotives. Eventually the rear trailing truck was adapted to allow for a larger firebox, along the same lines as expansion of the 2-8-0 from the 2-8-2. By the second decade of the century, the 2-10-2 had successfully adapted into a standard heavy road locomotive.

In the 1920s, Baldwin built some very fine examples of 2-10-2s for Southern Pacific, Great Northern, and other lines. SP's became particularly famous as a result of a clever publicity stunt by Samuel Vauclain, then president of Baldwin. In autumn 1921, SP had placed an unusually large order of 50 2-10-2s. At the time, America was suffering from economic doldrums, and Vauclain was keen on demonstrating that there would soon be a return to prosperity. So, with SP's acquiescence, Baldwin held back 20 of the new machines and then on May 26, 1922, dispatched them all at once to the West Coast in a special train called a "Prosperity Special." Their arrival coincided with July 4

SAMUEL M. VAUCLAIN: BALDWIN PERSONIFIED

Born with a passion for locomotives, Samuel M. Vauclain grew to be the man who best personified the Baldwin Locomotive Works during its later years of steam production. Born on May 18, 1856, Samuel was the ninth of ten children born to Andrew C. Vauclain and Mary A. Campbell. Samuel would follow the railroad path of his father, who had a varied career as a pioneer in the railroad industry. Andrew worked for Matthias W. Baldwin during the locomotive builder's formative years, serving as M. W. Baldwin's traveling engineer, among other positions. Later, he worked for Philadelphia & Reading in various capacities, serving for a while as the line's master mechanic. At the time of Samuel's birth, Andrew was employed by the Pennsylvania Railroad at its Altoona, Pennsylvania, shops, where he remained until retirement.

In 1872, Samuel began as an apprentice at the Altoona Shops. After five years, he completed his apprenticeship and joined the shops as a full-time paid railroad employee. In 1882, PRR sent him to Baldwin's Philadelphia works as an inspector for the railroad, and a year later Baldwin offered Samuel an important position at the works, which he accepted. The close relationship between the two Philadelphia-based companies made Samuel's employment at Baldwin mutually beneficial to the builder and the railroad. PRR remained one of Baldwin's best and most loyal customers.

Samuel's leadership skills, brilliant mind, and diligent work ethic allowed his rapid rise within the Baldwin organization. Equally important, Samuel was the right man at the right time. During the late nineteenth century Baldwin's production was growing rapidly as the company met a voracious demand for locomotives. Samuel began as superintendent of Baldwin's 17th Street Shops and by 1886 was general superintendent of the whole plant. Ten years later he was admitted as a Baldwin partner, and in 1911 he was made vice president of the Baldwin Locomotive Works. In May 1919, Samuel assumed the presidency of Baldwin, a position he held for nearly a decade. In 1929 he retired to the esteemed position of chairman of the board, which he held until his death in 1940.

Samuel's numerous achievements include important locomotive patents. His technological contributions to the company may best be remembered for his development of the four-cylinder symmetrical compound that bears his name (see Chapter 2). He was instrumental in Baldwin's decision to expand beyond its traditional Broad Street works in Philadelphia and oversaw the building of the sprawling Eddystone plant beginning in 1906. Yet, it was said that 22 years later, when Baldwin finally concluded its business at Broad Street, Samuel had tears in his eyes as he presided over the closure of the plant where he spent the majority of his career.

Samuel was a clever and astute salesman, and during the most difficult times he would personally call on railway leaders and heads of state. When he wanted Great Northern's business, he met with none other than James J. Hill and succeeded in convincing the Empire Builder to buy Baldwin engines. As part of Samuel's legacy, his charisma and personal attention to the people with whom he worked and did business were exceptional. When he secured orders for locomotives, he followed up with personal letters thanking the men who had ordered them. Yet Samuel remained closely in touch with the technical side of the business and had a thorough and detailed understanding of the machines his company designed and built. In 1926, he authored a detailed, insightful, and prophetic article on the future of diesel locomotives. His autobiography (co-written by Earl Chapin May), entitled *Steaming Up!*, was published in 1930. Among his many business, social, and humanitarian involvements, Samuel served as president of the Bryn Mawr Hospital near Philadelphia. His keen insight and technical knowledge combined with outstanding people skills made him one of the great business leaders of his generation.

Samuel M. Vauclain came to personify the Baldwin Locomotive Company of the early twentieth century. *Railroad Museum of Pennsylvania (PHMC)*

celebrations. In the January 1930 *Baldwin Locomotives*, Mark Noble describes the event as "the most notable train of railway motive power ever moved." Although most commonly used in freight service, SP's "Decks," as the 2-10-2s were known on the railroad, were initially assigned to passenger service over Donner Pass, replacing passenger-service Mallets.

During this same time frame, PRR was refining the older 2-10-0 into a modern heavy freight locomotive. Its Class I1s

Baldwin's famed *Prosperity Special* is ready to depart Eddystone on May 26, 1921. A Pennsylvania Railroad L1s Mikado leads a train of new Southern Pacific 2-10-2s bound for the West. Samuel Vauclain had a keen eye for publicity and took advantage of SP's large order of 2-10-2s to demonstrate that economic prosperity was returning to the United States after a short economic depression following World War I. *Baldwin image No. 8377, courtesy H. L. Broadbelt Baldwin Collection (RR88.2), Railroad Museum of Pennsylvania (PHMC)*

SPECIFICATIONS

Pennsylvania Railroad I1s*

Wheel arrangement: 2-10-0

Cylinders: Two 30½x32 in.

Drivers: 62 in.

Total engine weight: 386,100 lbs.

Tractive effort: 90,000 lbs.

* From *Baldwin Locomotives*, April 1925

This image is titled *Delivery of PRR Engine*. It was exposed in June 1923 and depicts Pennsylvania Railroad I1s No. 4471 on trial, probably on the grounds of Baldwin's Eddystone plant. Considered the ultimate development of the 2-10-0 Decapod, the type was refined by PRR when many other railroads were buying 2-10-2 Santa Fe types. PRR made good use of the type, working some right to the end of steam operations in 1957. Over the years, various figures have been given for the weight and tractive effort of PRR's I1s. *Baldwin image No. 8773-D, construction No. 56494, courtesy H. L. Broadbelt Baldwin Collection (RR88.2), Railroad Museum of Pennsylvania (PHMC)*

("s" for "superheated") is considered the ultimate development of this type. During 1922 and 1923, Baldwin built 475 I1s Decapods for PRR, which certainly contributed to the firm's prosperity. Known as "Hippos" because of their large boiler, these rode on 62-inch drivers and were designed for heavy freight service.

Lima's refining of the 2-10-4 Texas type for the Texas & Pacific pushed the 10-coupled type to new levels. Beginning in 1930, Santa Fe ordered a very large class of Texas-type models from Baldwin. Santa Fe's 5000 class were enormous machines that featured 74-inch drivers, 30x34-inch cylinders, and total engine weight of 545,000 pounds. These locomotives delivered an impressive 93,000 pounds tractive effort and produced 5,600 drawbar horsepower at 40 miles per hour. Reports estimate the piston thrust of the 5000 class machines at 210,000 pounds, the highest of any conventional locomotive ever built.

SUPERPOWER

Following World War I, American steam locomotives grew to impressive proportions. Despite the fundamental changes of the previous two decades, most American railroads in 1920 enjoyed robust, diverse, and, in many cases, growing traffic volumes.

A detailed view of the cylinder casting on a Pennsylvania Railroad Class I1s Decapod, designed with the unusual 30½ x 32–inch dimensions and worked at 250 psi. Specific to the I1s design was a 50 percent cutoff at maximum tractive effort to achieve improved fuel economy by taking greater advantage of the expansive steam power. *Baldwin Locomotives* magazine reported in January 1923 that, when working in full gear, the I1s piston valves had a steam lap of 2 inches and travel of 6 inches. Since this occasionally made it difficult to start the locomotive, the engineer controlled auxiliary starting ports. *Baldwin image No. 9409, courtesy H. L. Broadbelt Baldwin Collection (RR88.2), Railroad Museum of Pennsylvania (PHMC)*

Though the automotive industry was in its infancy, its early threat had encouraged locomotive builders and railroads to continue to refine specialized locomotives for fast and bulk freight and fast passenger operations during the 1920s and 1930s. Many of the most innovative new types were largely the work of Baldwin's competitors or were originated by railroad mechanical departments. Yet Baldwin benefited from innovations and built new types for many railroads. In some situations, completely new wheel arrangements were introduced, while in others locomotive design was refined to new performance plateaus using established wheel arrangements.

Lima introduced "superpower" types that were embraced by many railroads and ultimately built by all three major manufacturers. These locomotives featured sufficiently large fireboxes and boilers capable of supplying ample quantities of steam to enable the locomotives to maintain full power at sustained speeds—even when climbing long grades. Lima used a twin-axle trailing truck to support a substantially larger boiler, which, combined with other energy-saving innovations, resulted in substantially more powerful designs. Lima's first innovation was to expand the 2-8-2 into the 2-8-4 Berkshire type in 1924. Next, Lima developed the 2-10-4 Texas type, first built for Texas & Pacific. These were followed in 1927 by Alco's development of the 4-6-4 Hudson and 4-8-4 Northern types. (The Northern proved the most popular of the new wheel arrangements and was built for both fast freight and fast passenger services.) Baldwin was among the pioneers of the simple articulated. This type was the logical advancement of the Mallet articulated, but instead of using a compound arrangement, it used high-pressure steam to all cylinders.

As diesel locomotives became commercially available, Baldwin pushed the envelope of steam design and produced a variety of extreme locomotives aimed at matching or exceeding the capabilities of diesels. While these were some of the fastest and most powerful locomotives ever conceived, they quickly proved to be commercial failures when they could not match the economics of the diesel-electric. Although it may seem logical to state, steam rail reached its performance zenith in steam power's final years,

SPECIFICATIONS

New York, New Haven & Hartford I-5

Wheel arrangement: 4-6-4

Cylinders: Two 22x30 in.

Drivers: 80 in.

Total engine weight: 365,300 lbs.

Tractive effort: 44,000 lbs.

New Haven Railroad's last new passenger steam locomotives were the 10 Class I-5 4-6-4 Shoreliners built by Baldwin for service on New Haven's famous Shoreline Route between Boston and New Haven. *Baldwin image No. 11342, construction No. 61965, courtesy H. L. Broadbelt Baldwin Collection (RR88.2), Railroad Museum of Pennsylvania (PHMC)*

This artist's sketch portrays a proposed but never built streamlined 4-8-4 for Northern Pacific. It has hints of Southern Pacific's *Daylight* 4-8-4s and Milwaukee Road's late-era 4-8-4s. *Baldwin image No. 11977, courtesy H. L. Broadbelt Baldwin Collection (RR88.2), Railroad Museum of Pennsylvania (PHMC)*

SPECIFICATIONS

Great Northern No. 2031

Wheel arrangement: 2-8-8-2

Cylinders: Four 18x24 in.

Drivers: 63 in.

Total engine weight: 594,940 lbs.

Tractive effort: 127,000 lbs.

Great Northern 2031 was completed in June 1925 as part of an order for Class R-1 2-8-8-2 simple articulateds designed to move freight over the Continental Divide on the railroad's transcontinental main line. Unlike most earlier articulateds, these were not compounds; high-pressure steam was fed directly to all four cylinders. The locomotive operated for three decades before it was stored serviceable in August 1956. *Baldwin image No. 9563, construction No. 58481, courtesy H. L. Broadbelt Baldwin Collection (RR88.2), Railroad Museum of Pennsylvania (PHMC)*

The boiler for a Great Northern Class R-1 2-8-8-2 simple articulated is outside Eddystone on a flatcar. Key to the R-1's successful design was the boiler's even weight distribution on the engine frames. At the front of the boiler, a single bearing surface was intended to distribute weight evenly to minimize frame stress. Improved weight distribution was necessary because the R-1 simple articulated was built for higher speeds than older Mallet articulated types. *Baldwin image No. 9566, construction No. 58481, courtesy H. L. Broadbelt Baldwin Collection (RR88.2), Railroad Museum of Pennsylvania (PHMC)*

SPECIFICATIONS
Paulista de Estradas de Ferra No. 108

Wheel arrangement: 4-8-2

Cylinders: Three 17x22 in.

Drivers: 48 in.

Total engine weight: 171,500 lbs.

Tractive effort: 34,100 lbs.

Unusual among Baldwin's exports was an order for three-cylinder Mountain types built in 1925 for Brazil's Paulista de Estradas de Ferra. Where Alco made a business of selling three-cylinder simple types domestically in the 1920s, Baldwin only experimented with three-cylinder locomotives in the U.S. market. *Baldwin image No. 9675, construction No. 58859, courtesy H. L. Broadbelt Baldwin Collection (RR88.2), Railroad Museum of Pennsylvania (PHMC)*

but this pattern did not necessarily follow in other countries. The greatest steam locomotives to leave Baldwin were built alongside its new diesel-electric line.

DUPLEX

The 4-8-4 emerged as the most versatile of the superpower designs developed in the 1920s. Its combination of eight-coupled drivers with ample boiler capacity allowed the type to produce high tractive effort with great horsepower. For this reason, the 4-8-4 could be assigned to a great variety of mainline services, working fast freights and long passenger trains while serving in both level and graded territory. Baldwin was among the first to build the 4-8-4, constructing Santa Fe's 3751 class beginning in 1927. Baldwin and Santa Fe continued to refine the type, and by the mid-1930s the railroad had some of the finest 4-8-4s in

the United States. These were assigned to long runs up to 1,800 miles that crossed several divisions.

In the early 1930s, Baldwin aimed to improve upon the 4-8-4 by designing a "Duplex" locomotive with a divided drive on a rigid frame. This would use two complete sets of cylinders and running gear but without articulation. It was several years before Baldwin found a customer for its concept. A paper by Baldwin chief engineer Ralph P. Johnson entitled "The Four Cylinder Duplex Locomotive As Built for the Pennsylvania Railroad" explains the theory behind the planning, design, and construction of this unusual locomotive: "Four-cylinder locomotives have been common for years, but with articulated frames. Such engines, while powerful, were not suited to high speeds, since the front unit is not sufficiently stable as spring centering devices are not effective against slight lateral displacements. In addition, the

SPECIFICATIONS

Chesapeake & Ohio No. 1572

Wheel arrangement: 2-8-8-2

Cylinders: Four 23x33 in.

Drivers: 57 in.

Total engine weight: n/a

Tractive effort: n/a

Chesapeake & Ohio bought massive 2-8-8-2 simple engines from both Alco and Baldwin, with the latter delivering its share in 1926. *Baldwin image No. 9710, construction No. 58964, courtesy H. L. Broadbelt Baldwin Collection (RR88.2), Railroad Museum of Pennsylvania (PHMC)*

The safety valves lift on a Pennsylvania Railroad T1 are seen being tested, March 13, 1942. While Baldwin's experimental Duplex types were aimed at PRR, Baldwin hoped for a much wider market for this high-speed steam locomotive and to compete for sales with diesel-electrics, specifically Electro-Motive's E-unit. Despite the obvious advantages of diesel-electrics, in 1942 officials at Baldwin still believed they could make a case for steam. *Baldwin image No. 12160, courtesy H. L. Broadbelt Baldwin Collection (RR88.2), Railroad Museum of Pennsylvania (PHMC)*

hinged connection between front and rear units has always been a high maintenance item."

The primary advantage of non-articulated divided drive was to reduce piston stroke and lower the necessary weight of the drive rods. This lowered piston thrust and reciprocating weight, which was especially significant for high-speed runs, while maintaining high lateral stability and lowering maintenance costs.

Johnson notes that Baldwin proposed such a machine to Baltimore & Ohio as early as 1932, and then to Florida East Coast in 1935 and New Haven Railroad in 1936. In 1937, B&O built a locomotive inspired by Baldwin's concept but using one engine with rear-facing cylinders. This proved problematic for a variety of reasons.

Then in the late 1930s, Pennsylvania Railroad envisioned a new superpower steam locomotive that could outperform the latest passenger diesels and so teamed with the three large steam builders in an all-new design. What they came up with was PRR's famous S1, a Duplex type with fantastic proportions and great power, and dressed as a futuristic streamliner. This machine entertained visitors at the 1939 New York World's Fair where it moved continuously on a treadmill made of rollers. While thrilling to watch, the enormous locomotive proved impractical in actual road service because its long wheelbase restricted operation east of Pittsburgh. It was further limited because it was too long to fit on most turntables.

Not easily defeated by nominal oversights, PRR worked with Baldwin to design a more practical Duplex type with more reasonable proportions. By the time the railroad was ready to build its new Duplex, American involvement in World War II had resulted in strict limits on new locomotive designs, and PRR had to obtain special permission from the War Production Board to build a pair of experimental Duplex prototypes. Where the S1 had used a 6-4-4-6 wheel arrangement, Baldwin's new T1 prototypes featured the 4-4-4-4 wheel arrangement that was essentially an adaptation of the successful 4-8-4 Northern. These were intended for 100-mile-per-hour operation with an 880-ton passenger train. Unlike the S1, the T1's more manageable size conformed to most of the railroad's weight and length restrictions.

The two experimental T1 prototypes were styled with distinctive streamlined shrouds designed by Raymond Loewy, who gave the T1 a mean-looking "sharknose" profile—a design similar to that later adopted for Baldwin's road diesels. During the war, Baldwin and PRR put the railroad's T1 prototypes through extensive testing at Pennsy's Altoona test plant, one of the few scientific steam locomotive research facilities in the world. Meanwhile, the prototypes featured prominently in advertising that promoted the war effort and PRR's fantastic vision for the future of railroading. During the war, PRR published a brochure illustrated with color photographs that promoting the T1 prototypes: "They have been designed to do work in steam-operated territory corresponding to that done by the large electric locomotives, Class GG1, in electrified territory, thus avoiding the double-heading of heavy passenger trains. Their overall dimensions are such that they can be operated on any part of the main lines of the Pennsylvania System."

PRR deemed these prototypes successful and after the war ordered 50 T1s: 25 from its own Juniata shops in Altoona and another 25 from Baldwin. Production models had less-refined streamlining; although these retained the basic Loewy stylistic elements, they lacked the elegance of the prototypes. The tapered nose was less pronounced, and the shrouded skirting was minimized for ease of maintenance. Baldwin had hoped the PRR's order would result in interest from other railroads and that Duplex types might prove popular in the postwar environment. However, most postwar passenger power orders were for diesels, not steam, and certainly not for something as unusual as the Baldwin Duplex.

The T1 embodied all the features of the most modern steam: 80-inch drivers, roller bearings, high boiler pressure, and even recently developed poppet valves instead of more conventional piston valves. In terms of sheer speed, the T1 could outperform just about anything else on the road on level track. Unfortunately, the T1s suffered from poor reliability, and by the mid-1950s all had been sidelined.

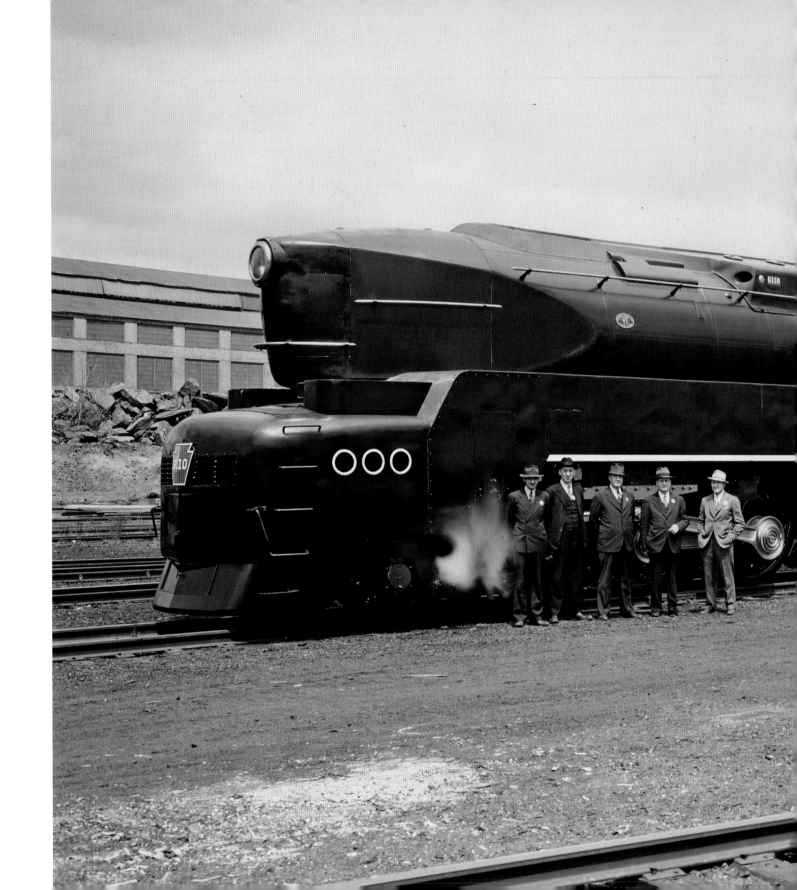

SPECIFICATIONS

Pennsylvania Railroad Prototype T1

Wheel arrangement: 4-4-4-4

Cylinders: Four 19¾x26 in.

Drivers: 80 in.

Total engine weight: 497,200 lbs.

Tractive effort: 65,000 lbs. (without booster)

Opposite: Color film was scarce during World War II, and 8x10-inch Kodachrome was especially hard to get, yet Baldwin made a series of images of its latest creation, prototype high-speed Duplex types for Pennsylvania Railroad. Officials pose with PRR T1 No. 6110 in 1942. *Courtesy Matt Gray Collection (RR95.2), Railroad Museum of Pennsylvania (PHMC)*

rods. Although built for fast freight and passenger service, the locomotive suffered from high fuel consumption and some reliability problems, and it was withdrawn from service after a few years.

In 1947–1948, Baldwin and Westinghouse jointly constructed three enormous streamlined steam-turbine-electrics for Chesapeake & Ohio passenger service. These featured a 4-8-0-4-8-4 wheel arrangement with 40-inch wheels. Each locomotive used a single Westinghouse turbine to power four direct current generators, which combined to deliver up to 6,000 horsepower for speeds up to 100 miles per hour. Each locomotive weighed a phenomenal 857,000 pounds. Not deemed successful, these very unusual machines operated in service for a very short time. A similar type of steam-turbine-electric, although less powerful at 4,500 horsepower and more conservatively styled, was built experimentally in 1954 for Norfolk & Western freight service. Named *Jawn Henry*, it operated for a couple of years alongside N&W's late-era Mallets and simple articulateds.

END OF STEAM

In November 1945, Baldwin chief engineer Ralph P. Johnson authored a paper entitled "Railroad Motive Power Trends" in which he analyzes and acknowledges various types of modern locomotives. By that time, Baldwin was firmly established as a builder of diesel switchers and had begun to sell commercial road diesels. Yet, Johnson remained naively optimistic regarding conventional steam, writing, "The ruggedness of the steam locomotive cannot be overlooked."

After addressing attempts to improve thermal efficiency, Johnson explains, "The steam locomotive will never make any dramatic increases in thermal efficiency but I am sure its steady improvement will continue. And I am also sure that the qualities that have made it popular heretofore will insure it a large place in future locomotive inventories."

Baldwin built its final domestic steam locomotives in 1948 and its last exports in 1950.

Constructed in 1944, Pennsylvania Railroad's Baldwin-built Class S2 No. 6200 was unique in several ways. It was the only direct-drive Baldwin steam turbine and the only steam locomotive ever built with a 6-4-6 wheel arrangement. It used two turbines: a large one for forward and a smaller one for reverse. Although relatively obscure in revenue service, the locomotive became familiar to thousands of children when Lionel reproduced it in O scale beginning in 1946. *Baldwin image No. 15024, courtesy H. L. Broadbelt Baldwin Collection (RR88.2), Railroad Museum of Pennsylvania (PHMC)*

TURBINES

Among Baldwin's final steam designs were a few steam turbines. These efforts followed experiments by various European railways, and in 1938, General Electric had built two very powerful steam-turbine-electrics for Union Pacific, which later tested on Great Northern but were dismantled during World War II.

Baldwin's first steam turbine was built for Pennsylvania Railroad in 1944. This unusually powerful locomotive had an enormous boiler and an unorthodox 6-8-6 wheel arrangement. PRR classed this machine S2, since its massive S1 Duplex had used a 6-4-4-6 arrangement. The S2 was particularly unusual among steam turbines because it used direct drive rather than electrical transmission. It had a pair of Westinghouse turbines, one rated at 6,900 horsepower for forward motion and a smaller 1,500-horsepower Westinghouse for reverse. It had 68-inch drive wheels coupled with conventional connecting

In 1947 and 1948, Baldwin built three large, experimental, streamlined, steam-turbine, electric locomotives for Chesapeake & Ohio's high-speed passenger service. Each locomotive delivered 6,000 horsepower using a Westinghouse non-condensing steam turbine that powered a pair of 1,000-kilowatt main generators using dual shafts and helical reduction gearing. As with Baldwin diesels, the traction motors were permanently connected in parallel. While among the most unusual passenger locomotives built in the United States, C&O's turbines were spectacularly unsuccessful. *Baldwin image No. 13430, courtesy H. L. Broadbelt Baldwin Collection (RR88.2), Railroad Museum of Pennsylvania (PHMC)*

Pennsylvania Railroad's prototype GG1 electric is seen under construction at Eddystone in 1934. Following difficulties with its P5-class electric that used the 2-C-2 arrangement, PRR built a pair of streamlined center-cab prototypes, the 2-C+C-2 GG1 pictured here and a 2-D-2 class R-1. Following PRR's intensive evaluation at Claymont, Delaware, in September 1934, the GG1 was selected as the railroad's new high-speed electric. For production locomotives, the body style was refined to include an all-welded design in place of riveted construction. This GG1 survives today at the Railroad Museum of Pennsylvania. *Baldwin image No. 16234, courtesy H. L. Broadbelt Baldwin Collection (RR88.2), Railroad Museum of Pennsylvania (PHMC)*

The desire to reduce locomotive maintenance costs, increase fuel efficiency, and realize better performance led railroads to investigate new motive power options. Since the early years of the twentieth century, a few railroads had invested in electrification. Initially, this was developed to comply with strict new air pollution regulations, notably in New York City. However, railroads found that electrification offered other advantages, including much greater energy efficiency, the ability to move much heavier trains with a single crew, and greatly simplified locomotive maintenance.

Because electric locomotives offered exceptionally high availability (i.e., were rarely out of service for repairs), low maintenance costs, and vastly superior tractive characteristics, the industry began to speculate that electrification might be

Among the most unusual images in the Baldwin archives are artists' sketches like this that depict locomotive designs that were never executed. This was one of several concepts for a streamlined body for Pennsylvania Railroad's P5 electric, probably dating from 1933–1934. *Courtesy H. L. Broadbelt Baldwin Collection (RR88.2), Railroad Museum of Pennsylvania (PHMC)*

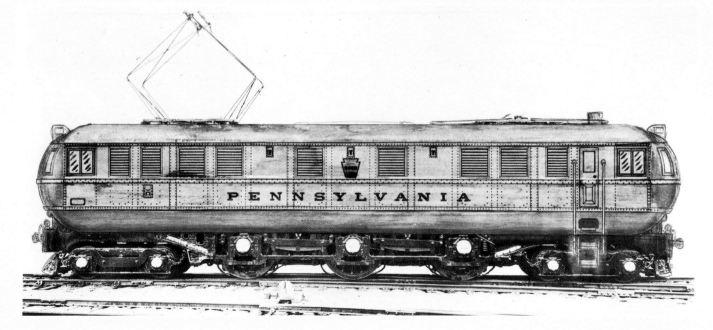

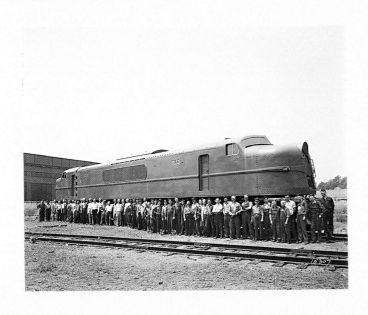

tion, ultimately wiring a total of 660 noncontiguous route miles in Montana, Idaho, and Washington.

Electrified operations never represented more than a tiny portion of the total American railroad mileage, remaining too costly for most railroads to consider as an effective motive-power solution. However, the industry's desire to take advantage of electric traction ultimately led to the development, refinement, and widespread adoption of diesel-electric motive power after World War II.

Baldwin, with its partner Westinghouse, was a pioneer in construction of heavy electrics. For the better part of six decades the Baldwin-Westinghouse partnership built electrics for American railroads and export. This represented a small yet important part of the Baldwin locomotive story, and many of the key electric designs were subjects of company photographers. Typically, these images were of half-finished locomotives waiting for shipping to Westinghouse for

During World War II, New Haven ordered 10 streamlined, double-ended electrics for freight service classed EF-3. Similar in appearance to the EP-4s built in the late 1930s by General Electric, the EF-3 order was divided evenly between GE and Baldwin-Westinghouse. This is the carbody for New Haven No. 0153. *Baldwin image No. 15307, courtesy H. L. Broadbelt Baldwin Collection (RR88.2), Railroad Museum of Pennsylvania (PHMC)*

the future for American railroads. However, exceptionally high initial costs of electrification, combined with new antitrust regulations that curtailed both the incentive and ability of railroads to invest in major capital projects, greatly limited implementation of heavy railroad electrification in the United States. Only in a few cases did railroads electrify mainlines.

New Haven Railroad was a pioneer of heavy mainline electrification and was the first to employ a high-voltage, alternating-current, overhead system. Various lines later adopted this system, including Pennsylvania Railroad, which ultimately operated the most extensive electrified network in the United States. Other lines adopted direct-current systems. New York Central pioneered an under-running third-rail system, but overhead direct-current was more common. Milwaukee Road installed the most extensive direct-current overhead mainline electrifica-

New Haven Railroad box-cab electric bodies await shipment to Westinghouse for installation of electrical gear. *Baldwin image No. 4157, courtesy H. L. Broadbelt Baldwin Collection (RR88.2), Railroad Museum of Pennsylvania (PHMC)*

A front view of Baldwin's diesel pioneer, No. 58501. In 1926, Baldwin experimented with this "oil-electric" powered by a 1,000-horsepower, two-cycle diesel engine, testing it in both road and switching service. *Baldwin image No. 9553, construction No. 58501, courtesy H. L. Broadbelt Baldwin Collection (RR88.2), Railroad Museum of Pennsylvania (PHMC)*

Opposite: This rare 8x10 Kodachrome image shows Baldwin's experimental road diesel, No. 6000. Designed and built during World War II, this was Baldwin's unorthodox approach to construction of a high-speed, 6,000-horsepower road diesel that emulated contemporary heavy electric locomotive practice. Using a modular design, it was to be powered by eight 408-series diesel engines, each with a separate main generator. The 6,000-horsepower, multi-engine concept quickly proved a dismal failure, and in 1945 No. 6000's iconic running gear was recycled for use on Seaboard Air Line's more conservatively powered No. 4500. *Baldwin image No. 15377-2, construction No. 64639, courtesy H. L. Broadbelt Baldwin Collection (RR88.2), Railroad Museum of Pennsylvania (PHMC)*

CHAPTER **FOUR**

DIESEL LOCOMOTIVES

ALTHOUGH BEST REMEMBERED for its steam locomotive excellence, Baldwin was by no means limited to steam production. Baldwin and Westinghouse had been successful partners in the construction of electric locomotives since the 1890s (see sidebar, Chapter 3), while Baldwin was among the pioneers of internal combustion–powered locomotives, having constructed small gasoline-mechanical locomotives beginning in 1910. The development of diesel-electric technology was a natural advancement of these technologies. In 1925, following the lead of the Alco–General Electric–Ingersoll-Rand consortium, Baldwin built an experimental "oil-electric" boxcab locomotive. At that time, Alco-GE-IR commercially offered 300-horsepower boxcab switchers,

primarily aimed at urban markets, where air-pollution regulations discouraged the use of steam locomotives. By contrast, Baldwin's experimental was intended to produce 1,000 horsepower and was designed for road service as well as switching, making it among the world's first road diesels.

Identified by construction number 58501 and designated as Class 12 (OE) 1000-1-CC 1, Baldwin's first diesel-electric locomotive was a unique creation, derived largely from the company's experience with heavy electric locomotives. It was powered by a Knudsen Motor Company water-cooled, two-cycle, 12-cylinder diesel built at Eddystone under license by Baldwin. Company literature indicates that cylinders were

9¾x13½ (diameter and stroke). A Westinghouse electrical system transmitted power to the wheels, and the locomotive used heavy A1A trucks (center axle unpowered) with powered axles connected to Westinghouse 353-D-3 motors. The machine measured 52 feet, 1¾ inches long over coupler faces and was 14 feet, 7 inches tall and 10 feet, 5 inches wide. It carried 750 gallons of fuel oil and weighed 275,000 pounds with 180,000 pounds on driving wheels. Air-actuated sanders were used to prevent drivers from slipping, and the locomotive was rated at 52,200 pounds starting tractive effort.

Based on these specifications, this was by far the most powerful diesel-electric constructed in the United States at that time, and significantly more powerful than those sold by Alco-GE-IR. The November 1925 *Railway Mechanical Engineer* offers a detailed profile, reporting that No. 58501 was tested in switching service on Reading Company and also assigned service trials on Reading's road freights. Here, working 40 miles between Reading and Tamaqua, Pennsylvania, the locomotive hauled freights weighing more than 1,000 tons up a 0.7 percent ascending grade at 16 miles per hour. Downgrade, it moved trains weighing more than 2,000 tons. Despite these nominal successes, the locomotive was never replicated. In their book *Baldwin Diesel Locomotives*, authors Gary and Stephen Dolzall note that 58501 suffered from an overly complex diesel engine design and spent the next eight years in relative obscurity as an Eddystone shop switcher. It was cut up for scrap in 1941.

Where the Alco-GE-IR consortium developed a moderate trade in boxcab switchers in the mid-1920s, Baldwin refrained from entering the market for commercial diesel locomotives at that time. This was a very specialized business, and despite Alco's foray, Baldwin focused the bulk of its locomotive production on design, construction, and sale of steam locomotives. It must be remembered that at this time, diesel engine design was still in its formative stages, and the relatively heavy engine blocks available yielded low horsepower per weight, making it impractical to consider designing high-output diesel locomotives to rival modern steam power.

VAUCLAIN'S DIESEL VISION

In July 1926, Baldwin president Samuel M. Vauclain published a detailed and insightful article in *Baldwin Locomotives* entitled "Internal Combustion Locomotives and Vehicles" in which he offers a comprehensive history of the diesel locomotive up to that moment and spells out a forward-looking approach regarding the future of diesel locomotive design. Vauclain profiles various diesel prototypes in the United States and Europe, and accurately analyzes the benefits and pitfalls of diesel-electrics as compared with steam locomotives while revealing a profound vision as to the future of American motive power. Early in his article he writes:

> *The Diesel* motor *shows an overall thermal efficiency as high as 33 percent, while steam* locomotive *performance is about ¼ of this figure. But even with this handicap, the steam locomotive of today is a remarkably flexible and reliable traveling power plant. In order to properly compete, no matter what the fuel economies may be, the internal combustion locomotive must approximate this same flexibility and reliability. It must have ease of control, ability to start a full tonnage train, and adaptability to the rapid change in physical conditions met in operation: such as variable speeds, gradients, curves, and weather conditions. It must not be too complicated in detail nor too heavy per horse-power developed. Herein then are the basic features which the designer must constantly bear in mind. While a gain in thermal efficiency will warrant an increase in initial cost, the price must not be so prohibitive as to offset the anticipated gain in cost of operation.*

Vauclain goes on in detail, describing the types of various experimental internal combustion engines and locomotives and their virtues, while comparing the various types of

SPECIFICATIONS
Baldwin No. 58501
Wheel arrangement: A1A-A1A
Engine: Knudsen two-cycle diesel
Horsepower: 1,000
Total engine weight: 275,000 lbs.
Starting Tractive effort: 52,200 lbs.

Baldwin No. 58501 was built in 1926 and had more in common with contemporary electrics of the period than with Baldwin's later diesel-electric line. *Baldwin image No. 9554, construction No. 58501, courtesy H. L. Broadbelt Baldwin Collection (RR88.2), Railroad Museum of Pennsylvania (PHMC)*

transmissions—mechanical, hydraulic, and electric—acknowledging that the electric transmission was best suited to heavy American-style operations. Toward the end, he profiles Baldwin's own 58501, illustrating the details of the equipment. In his conclusion, Vauclain admits the challenges facing development of the diesel locomotive, as well as some advantages of a feasible diesel-electric locomotive, writing:

> *. . . considerable time must elapse and many millions of dollars be expended in the development of an "oil-electric" power unit in the shape of a locomotive before machines of this type will figure to any great extent in transportation service. . . . If a machine as serviceable as the present steam locomotive and one that can be as economically maintained in service can be produced, then great relief and resulting economy will be obtained by the elimination of ash pits, the various ash-handling devices connected therewith, and the necessity for transferring refuse, as well as much of the periodical attention required to keep the ordinary steam locomotive in proper condition for service.*

Baldwin was not alone in its outlook and worked with Westinghouse in construction of several pioneering diesel-powered railway vehicles. Among these attempts was an experimental effort for Canadian National Railways in 1929 that John F. Kirkland describes in *Dawn of the Diesel Era* as a joint effort of the railway, Westinghouse, and Baldwin's affiliate Canadian Locomotive Company. Considered the first passenger diesel, it was powered by Beardmore diesel engines.

Yet, in the early years of diesel development, it was switching locomotives, not road power, that remained the primary focus of most diesel locomotive development. In 1929, Baldwin built a second experimental that was designed along the lines of a switching locomotive. Significantly this was awarded construction number 61000 and, like the 58501, was rated at 1,000 horsepower. Baldwin designated it as Class 8-(OE), 1000-1-CC, 1. This machine featured a decidedly different appearance than No. 58501, although it retained the dual-cab boxcab configuration. Powered by a German-designed six-cylinder Krupp diesel with 15x15-inch cylinders, No. 61000 rode on twin two-axle trucks with all axles powered in what would become the familiar B-B wheel arrangement (used by light electric trolley motors and established by the Alco-GE-IR diesels as a preferred diesel switching wheel arrangement) later adopted by the vast majority of American diesel switchers. This locomotive measured 51 feet long and 15 feet, 8¾ inches tall. At 270,000 pounds, Baldwin No. 61000 weighed slightly less than No. 58501, but since all of its axles were powered, No. 61000 placed greater adhesive weight on drivers and delivered greater tractive effort, 67,500 pounds. For a switching locomotive, high tractive effort at low speed is desirable.

Baldwin sent No. 61000 on an extensive tour, where it was tested by Illinois Central, Milwaukee Road, Nickel Plate Road, Northern Pacific, Oliver Iron Mining, Pennsylvania Railroad, Rock Island Lines, and Santa Fe. Unfortunately, Baldwin's debut of this experimental was ill-timed as economic shockwaves stemming from the October 1929 stock market crash soon dried up the new locomotive market, leaving few buyers for locomotives of any kind. Despite the relative success of No. 61000, it would be nearly another decade before Baldwin would enter the commercial diesel locomotive market.

DEPRESSION-ERA DIESEL DEVELOPMENTS

The Great Depression presented one of the worst climates for locomotive sales in decades, yet it also resulted in a series of developments that forever changed the North American locomotive business. Although Baldwin hesitated to make

This unusual action photograph shows Baldwin experimental diesel-electric No. 61000 at work and offers a detailed view of the top of the locomotive not available in the more common side-view builder's photographs. This was Baldwin's second diesel-electric, completed in May 1929. If the stock market crash in October of that year hadn't precipitated the Great Depression, would Baldwin have found resources to develop its diesel-electric line ahead of Electro-Motive? *Baldwin image No. 10371-B, construction No. 61000, courtesy H. L. Broadbelt Baldwin Collection (RR88.2), Railroad Museum of Pennsylvania (PHMC)*

In June 1939, just prior to beginning regular production of its standard diesel switchers, Baldwin completed this experimental switcher for Reading Company. It initially carried road number 36, as seen in this image inside the plant at Eddystone. The locomotive was equipped with the Baldwin-designed Batz cast-steel, two-axle trucks and featured a distinctive hood style. According to Gary and Stephen Dolzall, it was the test for a fabricated frame design. By contrast, Baldwin's production switchers used cast-steel frames through 1950. Kirkland lists this as a Baldwin Class 8-DE-660/1E. *Baldwin image No. 16628-6, construction No. 62300, courtesy H. L. Broadbelt Baldwin Collection (RR88.2), Railroad Museum of Pennsylvania (PHMC)*

16628.6

the necessary investment noted by Vauclain's 1926 article, another organization followed through with his plan. During this time diesel locomotive technology was rapidly advanced by the Electro-Motive Corporation, which soon developed as Baldwin's foremost competitor.

In 1930, automotive giant General Motors acquired the Winton Engine Company and one of its primary customers, Electro-Motive, a small design company that in the 1920s earned a solid reputation in the field of internal combustion railcars. Intensive investment by General Motors in the mid-1930s enabled Electro-Motive Corporation (Electro-Motive Division after 1940) to refine the Winton diesel engine design into a lightweight, high-output, and extraordinarily reliable locomotive powerplant. At the same time, EMC developed a variety of new locomotive configurations using a blend of railcar and automotive technologies. Through intensive research and development and applying new materials stemming from improved metallurgy, innovative fuel-injection technologies, and rapid-assembly/mass-production techniques, Electro-Motive, by the end of the decade, was able to offer reliable, mass-produced, high-output diesel-electric locomotives in several key configurations to rival modern steam locomotives from established manufacturers.

Electro-Motive's earliest efforts were in streamlined diesel power-cars for lightweight articulated trains. It rapidly expanded its market with a line of switchers in 1935, high-speed passenger diesels (E-units) in 1937, and high-horsepower road freight diesels (F-units) at the end of 1939. Although Electro-Motive diesels required greater capital investment than steam, they offered significant improvements in overall efficiency, reliability, and availability, while requiring substantially less maintenance. Electro-Motive had ticked all the boxes illustrated by Vauclain in his 1926 article, and it did this largely before Baldwin was ready with its first commercial diesel switchers.

In 1931, Baldwin acquired established engine manufacturers I. P. Morris and De La Vergne, moves equivalent to Alco's acquisition of the McIntosh & Seymour Engine Company two years earlier and GM's acquisition of Winton in 1930. De La Vergne had been building internal combustion engines for nearly four decades and was among the first licensees of the diesel engine, having constructed diesels since 1917. Baldwin transferred the company's production to its massive Eddystone plant and initiated locomotive engine development. Despite these moves and Vauclain's prophetic visions, Baldwin was slow to organize design and construction of a commercial diesel line and suffered from a lack of adequate financial backing.

Alco reacted to Electro-Motive by improving its diesel switcher design in the late 1930s, and by 1940 it was offering a road diesel similar to Electro-Motive's while aiming to develop a more competitive diesel engine. While Alco was reestablishing its commercial switcher business and Baldwin's electric locomotive partner, Westinghouse, was producing commercial diesel-electrics at its East Pittsburgh plant, Baldwin was just getting started in diesel-switcher development. Except for a handful of experimental types, Baldwin's first commercial diesel switchers were not ready for production until mid-1939, and the company didn't begin developing road locomotive designs until the early 1940s. Baldwin was reasonably successful with its switchers, but it didn't achieve great successes with its road diesels. During the 1930s, the company's diesel development fell far behind that of Electro-Motive, and by 1940 Baldwin was at a distinct disadvantage in the diesel market.

After World War II, the market for locomotives was at its most robust point in decades, presenting ample opportunity for all builders to enjoy a share of sales. In his book *From Steam to Diesel*, Albert Churella analyzes the builders' varying business practices. Where Electro-Motive mass-produced diesel-electrics in a fashion similar to the way parent GM built automobiles—establishing standard product lines and focusing production on a handful of basic types—Baldwin built diesels the same way it continued to build steam locomotives: in small, customized batches. Baldwin made an effort to standardize components among various types, but concurrent efforts to refine designs and offer a great variety of road diesel types for various service requirements—often making significant design changes for small production runs to suit individual customers—resulted in considerably more variation over much smaller production runs than its competitors. For

SPECIFICATIONS

Baldwin VO660 (0-4-4-0 1000/1DE)

Wheel arrangement: B-B

Engine: Six-cylinder Model VO

Horsepower: 660

Total engine weight: 195,500 lbs.

Starting Tractive effort: 50,000 lbs. (25 percent adhesion)

This 660-horsepower unit was the first production unit built to Baldwin's standard switcher specifications. Lettered for the Baldwin Locomotive Works and numbered 299 (foreshortened from its builder's number), this unit, according to John F. Kirkland, was dressed in light blue with gold lettering, and the company assigned it as an Eddystone plant switcher, where it also served as a demonstration model. Hood styling is representative of early Baldwin production switchers; it features an oval front radiator grille and curved valances. Later VO-powered switchers embodied simplified and more utilitarian styling. *Baldwin image No. 15316, construction No. 62299, courtesy H. L. Broadbelt Baldwin Collection (RR88.2), Railroad Museum of Pennsylvania (PHMC)*

the observer, this produced a great variety of unusual and eclectic locomotives, but it did little to forward Baldwin's reputation. High engineering costs, lower unit reliability, and low profit per unit put Baldwin at a serious disadvantage in the postwar diesel market.

DE LA VERGNE'S VO ENGINE

Under Baldwin's wing, De La Vergne developed a powerful four-cycle diesel specifically for locomotive applications. The Model VO engine featured cylinders 12¾ inches in diameter with a 15½-inch stroke and one intake valve and one exhaust valve per cylinder. Low idle speed was 250 rpm, and maximum throttle speed was 625 rpm—much slower than comparable engines designed by McIntosh & Seymour and Winton. The engine's A-frame block is described in the July 1940 *Diesel Railway Traction* as made from a welded-steel breastplate featuring "heavy transverse webs to support the bearings." Likewise, the welded frame incorporated "both the crankcase and cylinder block," while stress-relieved cast-iron wet liners were inserted into the cylinder block.

In 1939, Baldwin began mass production of diesel-electric locomotives by offering two switchers powered by six- and eight-cylinder VO engines rated at 660 and 1,000 horsepower, respectively. In the 1940s, Baldwin VO-powered diesel switchers are under construction in the tender shop at Eddystone. Notice the steam locomotive tenders at the top right of the image. Sheetmetal construction of diesel hoods was similar to work for steam locomotive tenders. *Baldwin image No. 16466, courtesy H. L. Broadbelt Baldwin Collection (RR88.2), Railroad Museum of Pennsylvania (PHMC)*

A Bosch solid fuel-injection system was employed with individual pumps and injectors for each cylinder. Pistons were of an aluminum flat-top design. Of special significance to the VO design was its unusual, patented cast hemispherical combustion chamber intended to improve performance and fuel economy.

SWITCHERS

Baldwin's first market for diesels, and by far its greatest diesel-locomotive success, was in the production and sale of switchers. By the mid-1930s, American railroads recognized the distinct cost and operational advantages associated with diesel switching operations. An article in the February 1940 *Baldwin Locomotives* entitled "Economics of Motive Power for Switching Service" quantifies these advantages:

. . . high starting torque, high acceleration in low speed range, greater visibility for the locomotive operator (engineer), high locomotive availability and lower maintenance costs, no objectionable smoke admissions, no requirements for coal,

water and ash handling facilities, greater crew comfort, the ability to use two or more locomotives together with a single crew, no standby losses [when the diesel is not in use it can be shut down], and lower fuel costs.

The ability of the diesel to apply full power from a start, combined with lower operating and maintenance costs, was a strong incentive for railroads to consider diesel switchers, and many lines across the country made their first diesel switcher acquisitions in the 1930s.

In the mid-1930s, as it refined its diesel designs, Baldwin produced a handful of experimental switchers. Finally, in 1939, it introduced its first standard diesel switcher line for regular commercial production. All of Baldwin's commercial switchers adhered to the end-cab hood type with the B-B

SPECIFICATIONS
Baldwin VO1000 (0-4-4-0 1000/1DE)
Wheel arrangement: B-B
Engine: Eight-cylinder Model VO
Horsepower: 1,000
Total engine weight: 240,000 lbs.
Starting Tractive effort: 60,000 lbs. (25 percent adhesion)

Atlantic Coast Line VO1000 (0-4-4-0 1000/1DE) diesel switcher No. 606 was completed at Eddystone in January 1942. It was photographed on 8x10-inch Kodachrome in a moment of sun on an otherwise overcast January day. During the war, Baldwin's commercial diesel production was limited to switchers, which were the only diesel types it had developed prior to American involvement in the conflict. *Baldwin image No. 12200, construction No. 64266, courtesy H. L. Broadbelt Baldwin Collection (RR88.2), Railroad Museum of Pennsylvania (PHMC)*

Female workers with a VO-powered switcher built for Baltimore & Ohio. A labor shortage during World War II resulted in many women assuming jobs traditionally held by men. *Baldwin image No. 16488-3, construction No. 70115, courtesy H. L. Broadbelt Baldwin Collection (RR88.2), Railroad Museum of Pennsylvania (PHMC)*

wheel arrangement established by Westinghouse and Alco in the early 1930s (and adopted by Electro-Motive in 1935). Both Alco and Electro-Motive offered switchers in the 600–660 horsepower and 900–1,000 horsepower ranges, so Baldwin followed this pattern, offering standard 660-horsepower and 1,000-horsepower models.

Outwardly, Baldwin's two types appeared similar and used most of the same equipment. Both were powered by normally aspirated variations of the De La Vergne VO diesel the 660-horse-power switcher with six cylinders and the 1,000-horsepower model with eight cylinders. Although most period Baldwin publications simply refer to these locomotives as "660 hp" and "1000 hp" diesel switchers, they have been retroactively classified by locomotive chroniclers as the "VO660" and "VO1000" models, which helps distinguish these types from the later Baldwin switchers. However, Baldwin does not appear to have used these designations in either its internal documents or promotional literature from the period.

Baldwin specifications indicate that the VO660 unit had a maximum speed of 45 miles per hour, and total weight in working order was approximately 198,500 pounds, giving it 50,000 pounds starting tractive effort (based on 25 percent adhesion). The VO1000 was rated for 60 miles per hour, weighed 240,000 pounds, and provided 60,000 pounds tractive effort. The VO1000's fuel tank had a 700-gallon capacity, compared with the VO660's 600 gallons. The VO660 was 45 feet long, and the VO1000 48 feet long; proportionately, the VO660 featured a 30-foot-6-inch wheelbase, while the VO1000 had a 33-foot-6-inch wheelbase. Both were 14 feet, 6 inches tall as measured to the top of the cab, while the hoods were 12 feet, 3⅛ inches tall, which allowed for good visibility.

In its early days, Electro-Motive offered a choice of either cast or welded fabricated frames on its switchers, but by 1940 it tended toward fabricated frames. In contrast, most of Baldwin's switchers and many of its later locomotive types were built with cast frames years after this style of construction had fallen out of favor with other builders. Baldwin's cast frames were produced by its General Steel Castings affiliate. A GSC ad in the 1947 *Locomotive Cyclopedia* highlights the advantages and virtues of this type of construction:

> *The one-piece cast steel construction makes it possible to distribute the metal to the best possible advantage and permits designing the under frame for the greatest strength with minimum weight. . . . The Commonwealth one-piece under frame provides an ideal foundation for the power plant, and*

accurately machined surfaces insure correct alignment of supports for [the] power plant. . . . [The frame's] rugged construction is valuable insurance against damage to the power plant in accidents.

The ad elaborated that the great strength inherent to the cast-frame design eliminated the need for joints and required less maintenance compared with other types of frame construction.

There were several variations of the VO types. A few early VO switchers were built with the unusual Batz-style truck, with wheels and axles made by Baldwin subsidiary Standard Steel Works. However, most used the common twin-axle, twin-motor, AAR-style A truck common on other builders' switchers of the period. The early VO models featured a pronounced pointed front end and a large ovular front air-intake grille, while later units featured a more flattened front end and a rectangular grille. The earlier units also featured curved valances connecting the cab with the running boards, superfluous styling that was eliminated on later production units. Based on statistics published in Louis A. Marre's *Diesel Locomotives: The First 50 Years*, between 1939 and 1946 Baldwin produced 142 VO660s and 548 VO1000s for North American railroads.

POSTWAR SWITCHERS

After World War II, Baldwin revised the De La Verne engine to correct for design defects and to allow for turbocharging, while making modifications to its switcher line that resulted in the improved DS-4-4-6 and DS-4-4-10 models being sold from 1946 to 1950. Initially these were powered by the recently introduced six-cylinder 606NA and eight-cylinder 608NA engines, respectively. The new locomotives shared common qualities with the VO models, though the new engines were intended to overcome design inadequacies of the VO engine types. In 1948, Baldwin offered the turbocharged, six-cylinder 606SC diesel in place of the 608NA engine (both were rated at 1,000 horsepower). In 1949, Baldwin upped the output of the normally aspirated, six-cylinder 606NA engine from 660 to 750 horsepower, which resulted in the DS-4-4-7.5 replacing the DS-4-4-6 model.

In 1950, Baldwin revised its locomotive line again, introducing another family of improved De La Vergne engines and further refining its locomotive designs. From 1950 to 1956, it built the 800-horsepower S-8 switcher powered by the six-cylinder, normally aspirated 606 diesel, and the S-12 powered by the six-cylinder, 1,200-horsepower, turbocharged 606A diesel. Externally there were only minor differences in the general appearance of these switchers. After 1950, Baldwin moved toward fabricated frames that were standard in the industry, though some units continued to be built with cast frames.

SWITCHER SUCCESS

Baldwin had recognized the superiority of the diesel switcher to steam early enough to refine and perfect its designs for satisfactory commercial applications. During World War II, Baldwin benefited from War Production Board directives (in place between 1942 and 1945) that largely limited its (and Alco's) diesel locomotive production to established standard switcher models while focusing Electro-Motive's efforts on road locomotives. Directives also restricted implementation of new designs and authorized construction of steam locomotives when materials needed for diesel locomotives were deemed of greater importance for military applications. The WPB's policies ensured that a relatively large number of Baldwin diesels found their way into American railroad fleets. Many of these survived for their expected life spans and longer. Baldwin's VO switchers remained common on American railroads through the 1960s, and some railroads continued to operate them longer. After the war, Baldwin's switchers remained its strongest diesel products (it sold more than 1,200 switchers in the postwar North American market), and switchers were among the last diesels to leave its Eddystone works. Even in 2009, a few of these old machines survive in service.

ROAD-SWITCHERS

The multiple-application road-switcher seems like a natural outgrowth of the diesel-electric switcher. Where early diesel

Missouri-Kansas-Texas bought 15 Baldwin-Lima-Hamilton S-12 switchers built in 1951 and 1952. These 1,200-horsepower units were powered by the six-cylinder 606A diesel. The model was one of Baldwin's most successful diesel types, and more than 450 units were built. Baldwin image No. 14264-6, construction No. 75510, courtesy H. L. Broadbelt Baldwin Collection (RR88.2), Railroad Museum of Pennsylvania (PHMC)

types were built to serve specific applications as largely defined by established steam locomotive types, the road-switcher crossed established service requirements to offer a greater level of versatility than possible with any one type of steam locomotive. Alco was first to develop the road-switcher type. In 1941, it expanded upon its 1,000-horsepower switcher, building a similar unit on a longer frame with road trucks for Rock Island's branch-line service. This type was intended to work both freight and passenger trains, while being able to switch sidings and serve on the main line. Later designated as the RS-1, this type was further developed during World War II for army applications and built in various configurations for service overseas.

Baldwin recognized the advantages of the road-switcher format and, after the war, offered a potpourri of configurations aimed at both domestic and export applications. While its first road-switchers were intended for export, it secured domestic road-switcher orders in 1946.

Baldwin's 1,000-horsepower DRS-4-4-1000 followed the pattern established by Alco's RS-1, essentially building a switcher on a longer frame with space for a steam generator under a short hood. (Since most road-switcher types were asymmetrical, "short" and "long" are used to describe the lengths of their two hoods.) The DRS-4-4-1000 was powered by Baldwin's 606SC engine. The first models were ordered by Tennessee Central in 1947 and constructed in 1948. These were followed by orders from Canadian Pacific and Pennsylvania Railroad that wrapped up production of this relatively obscure model at just 22 units. An export variation with A1A trucks sold greater numbers.

In 1950, when Baldwin improved its diesel line with the 606-series engines, it replaced the DRS-4-4-1000 with the new RS-12. This was nearly identical in its external appearance but was nominally more powerful at 1,200 horsepower. Baldwin sold 46 of this type. The combined sales of these two models represented a poor showing for Baldwin—during a 19-year production run, Alco's comparable RS-1 sold more than 400 units to lines in North America.

Many of Baldwin's diesel customers were involved in industries that required switching engines. Armco Steel Corporation was a repeat customer, buying several switchers over the years, including this Baldwin-Lima-Hamilton 800-horsepower Model S-8 in 1954, originally built for the Oliver Iron Mining Company. *Baldwin image No. 14457-3, construction No. 75834, courtesy H. L. Broadbelt Baldwin Collection (RR88.2), Railroad Museum of Pennsylvania (PHMC)*

More successful, and more significant, were Baldwin's heavy road-switchers, initially rated at 1,500 horsepower and powered with the 608SC engine. Baldwin offered this type in three basic configurations with four-motor B-B or A1A trucks, or six-motor C-C trucks, which were respectively designated as models DRS-4-4-1500, DRS-6-4-1500, and DRS-6-6-1500. These could be ordered with options for a steam generator or dynamic brakes and were sold both domestically and overseas. Baldwin's first domestic order for a 1,500-horsepower road-switcher was to Mississippi's Columbus & Greenville, a 168-mile east–west bridge line connecting its namesake points. DRS-6-4-1500, No. 601, was delivered in autumn 1946.

Baldwin had envisioned road-switcher customers would be railroads seeking powerful units with light axle weight for lines like the C&G. According to authors Gary W. Dolzall

and Stephen F. Dolzall in their book *Diesels from Eddystone: The Story of Baldwin Diesel Locomotives*, Baldwin's unit was the first 1,500-horsepower road-switcher built for North American service. The locomotive rode on A1A trucks and weighed 280,000 pounds with 187,000 pounds on drivers (23.4 tons per axle). Although A1A-equipped road-switchers would not develop as a common type, Alco's first sale of a 1,500-horsepower road-switcher, about the same time as Baldwin's, was also an A1A-equipped type (model RSC-2). As it transpired, these early orders played little bearing on total output, and A1A road-switchers turned out to be very specialized and highly unusual motive power on American rails. Far more common were mass-produced B-B, and in later years C-C, road-switchers, deemed better suited for most applications. Yet, Baldwin didn't enjoy especially robust road-switcher sales

Although the company had placed an order for Baldwin Centipedes, Union Pacific canceled the locomotives prior to delivery, and the railroad ended up owning very few Baldwin road diesels. Baldwins on UP's roster included six AS-616s, with DS No. 1261 pictured here. These were delivered in 1951–1952, and Gary and Stephen Dolzall note that all were traded to Electro-Motive for new diesels in 1968–1969. *Baldwin image No. 14271-2, construction No. 75186, courtesy H. L. Broadbelt Baldwin Collection (RR88.2), Railroad Museum of Pennsylvania (PHMC)*

with any of its initial offerings. Accordingly, Marre's totals for its B-B DRS-4-4-1500 indicate just 32 units sold between 1947 and 1950, with 29 units for the A1A DRS-6-4-1500.

The best-selling of these early Baldwin road-switchers was its DRS-6-6-1500 equipped with a C-C truck that accounted for 82 units. This model appears significant today because it was *the* pioneering domestic application of a six-motor road-switcher. While, in the 1940s, the high-tractive-effort, six-motor road-switcher was a specialized machine, over the next four decades this locomotive configuration became predominant over all other locomotive types. Today, the vast majority of locomotives bought new are C-C road-switchers.

Initially only Baldwin and Alco offered six-motor road-switchers. It wasn't until the early 1950s that Electro-Motive added this model type to its standard catalog. Unfortunately for Baldwin, although it pioneered this important type, it didn't enjoy brisk sales of six-motor road-switchers. They only emerged as the preferred type after Baldwin exited the market. Today, we can recognize the significance of Baldwin's innovation. Although Alco built 1,000-horsepower RS-1s with six-motor trucks for army applications during the war, Baldwin was first to sell six-motor types to domestic carriers; C&NW's acquisition of three DRS-6-6-1500s in 1948 marked the first application of six-motor road-switchers in America.

SPECIFICATIONS
Baldwin DRS-6-4-1500

Wheel arrangement: A1A-A1A

Engine: 608SC

Horsepower: 1,500

Total engine weight: 270,000 lbs.

Starting tractive effort: 55,950 lbs. (based on 30 percent adhesion)

Continuous tractive effort: 42,800 lbs. at 10.5 mph with 15:63 gearing

Baldwin's first domestic road-switcher order was in 1946 with the Columbus & Greenville for five DRS-6-4-1500s. Locomotive No. 601 was delivered in October, and Baldwin built the remainder of the order over the next few months. Today, this seems significant because of the crucial role played by road-switchers in American dieselization, however, at the time these locomotives were an unusual, specialized type. *Baldwin image No. 16535, construction No. 72626, courtesy H. L. Broadbelt Baldwin Collection (RR88.2), Railroad Museum of Pennsylvania (PHMC)*

Wheel arrangement: B-B

Engine: 608SC

Horsepower: 1,500

Total engine weight: 254,000 lbs.

Starting tractive effort: 76,200 lbs. (based on 30 percent adhesion)

Continuous tractive effort: 42,800 lbs. at 10 mph with 15:63 gearing

Western Maryland was one of nine customers for Baldwin's DRS-4-4-1500. It bought three of the model built in 1947 and 1948, and another four of the similar AS-16 introduced in 1950. Although Baldwin was among the first to produce heavy four-axle road-switchers, it didn't capture a large portion of this market. Combined production of the DRS-4-4-1500 and AS-16 was just 159 units, compared with more than 1,900 Alco RS-2 and RS-3s, which shared the same essential configuration and were built during the same time frame. Electro-Motive sold more than 2,700 GP7s and more than 4,200 GP9s. *Baldwin image No. 16662-2, construction No. 73399, courtesy H. L. Broadbelt Baldwin Collection (RR88.2), Railroad Museum of Pennsylvania (PHMC)*

Baldwin's new diesel line of 1950 resulted in slightly more powerful road-switchers with models AS-16 on B-B trucks, AS-416 on A1A trucks, and AS-616 on C-C trucks taking the place of older models. All were powered by the new 608A eight-cylinder, turbocharged diesel. The Baldwin-Westinghouse *Diesel-Electric General Specification for Standard Units* brochure published in July 1950 highlighted each of the new models being offered, including the road-switchers, noting improvements to its new line and addressing concerns with

earlier products: "Horsepower ratings have been increased throughout the entire line, and higher tractive effort ratings or continuous rated speed, or both, are now available in all models. This constitutes the first major revision on all Baldwin-Westinghouse locomotives since the war."

The brochure provided a detailed listing of specifications and performance characteristics for each locomotive. The four-motor AS-16 weighed 236,000 pounds with full adhesive weight on drivers, and it was rated at 59,000 pounds tractive effort (based upon

Not all Baldwin diesel photos were made on 8x10 film at Eddystone. For this image, Kodak 120 slide film was used to capture Union Railroad DRS-6-6-1500 No. 622 at work in the Pittsburgh area. The photographer wasn't well versed on diesel models. Mixed in with his images of six-motor Baldwin diesels in the Baldwin archive is a stray photo of an Alco RS-2. Someone at Baldwin was aghast, identifying the photo in bold marker as "Alco!" *Baldwin image No. 14629-5, construction No. 74698, courtesy H. L. Broadbelt Baldwin Collection (RR88.2), Railroad Museum of Pennsylvania (PHMC)*

25 percent adhesion). This gave the locomotive 59,000 pounds axle weight. The four-motor AS-416 weighed 252,000 pounds, delivered 43,500 pounds tractive effort (25 percent adhesion), and had a 43,500-pound axle weight (the similarity between tractive effort and axle weight figures appears to be coincidental). Baldwin's AS-616 put its full 325,000 pounds on drivers for 81,250 pounds tractive effort (25 percent adhesion) and 54,167 pounds axle weight. Where the two four-motor types were rated at 9.2 miles per hour maximum continuous speed with 52,500 pounds continuous tractive effort, the six-motor was capable of maintaining 6 miles per hour with 78,750 pounds continuous tractive effort. In other words, the six-motor AS-616 had outstanding hauling characteristics, which proved out in service as the big Baldwins earned a reputation as good "luggers," meaning they could move great tonnage at very slow speeds.

The AS-616 proved to be one of Baldwin's most popular road diesels, and 175 units were sold to lines in North America, including a handful of cab-less B units to Southern Pacific. Among the advantages of the diesel-electric versus steam is the ability for two or more units to work together in multiple from a common throttle, allowing railroads to adjust the amount of power assigned to a train easily without changing crew size. When operating in multiple, Baldwin AS-616s proved very capable. As a result, a few of the type enjoyed relatively long lives working heavy trains.

Baldwin's four-motor types didn't sell as well (the AS-16 sold just 127 units). This model was comparable to Alco's RS-3 road-switcher that accounted for more than 1,300 units, and Electro-Motive's GP7/GP9, which together sold approximately 7,000 units in the North American market between 1949 and 1958. Although late to develop road-switchers, Electro-Motive enjoyed the bulk of the sales as a result of the type's inherent versatility, combined with Electro-Motives' high-reliability, well-executed plan for component compatibility between models, and relatively low maintenance costs compared with the other builders.

TRANSFER LOCOMOTIVES

Among the specialized models developed by Baldwin were center-cab transfer-service locomotives. Although the company was neither the first nor the only company to build this relatively unusual variety, it was by far the most successful. The transfer locomotive was a heavy center-cab type designed for high

In addition to the standard AS-616, Southern Pacific ordered an anomalous variation of the type without cabs. While cab-less boosters were built as standard carbody diesels, cab-less road-switchers were uncommon, and SP's six-motor cab-less Baldwin-Lima-Hamiltons were very unusual. *Baldwin image No. 14245-18, construction Nos. 75227 and 75230, courtesy H. L. Broadbelt Baldwin Collection (RR88.2), Railroad Museum of Pennsylvania (PHMC)*

tractive effort and slow-speed freight services, and originally conceived to move long cuts of freight cars between yards. Baldwin's initial order for the type came from the Chicago area's Elgin, Joliet & Eastern, which ordered a single 2,000-horsepower unit in 1946. EJ&E No. 100 was powered by a pair of 1,000-horsepower 608NA engines—one under each hood at each end of the locomotive. This novel locomotive was featured in both *Railway Age* and *Diesel Railway Traction*, which noted its specifications for pulling ability and offered analyses of the relative costs compared with the 2-8-2 steam locomotives the diesel was designed to replace. Highlighted was the diesel's haulage of a freight train between East Joliet, Illinois, and Gary, Indiana, that consisted

of 69 cars (43 loads and 26 empties) weighing roughly 3,450 tons. On another occasion, it moved a 96-car loaded coal train weighing approximately 6,375 tons from the Pennsylvania Railroad interchange at Hartsdale, Indiana, to Gary. Both of these runs were on roughly level track. More telling of its abilities was the run from Waukegan, Illinois, toward Joliet, where a 1 percent climb away from Lake Michigan limited the hauling abilities of EJ&E's Mikado-type steam locomotives. Here, on one occasion, the center-cab diesel lifted an 88-car freight (37 loads and 51 empties) weighing an estimated 3,250 tons. On this grade, EJ&E determined that this diesel could take twice the tonnage as a Mikado. Performance was just part of the

Baldwin built this DT-6-6-2000 as a demonstrator in 1948. It was among the most powerful single-unit freight diesels sold in the immediate postwar market. This unit was later sold to Santa Fe, becoming its No. 2606, the seventh of its Baldwin transfer diesels. *Baldwin image No. 13710-4, construction No. 73980, courtesy H. L. Broadbelt Baldwin Collection (RR88.2), Railroad Museum of Pennsylvania (PHMC)*

equation, and EJ&E estimated that the diesel's repair costs were
just 24 cents per mile as compared with 40 cents for steam. Such
cost analysis needs qualification: at the time of the comparison,
EJ&E's 2-8-2s were an average of 26 years old. The diesel was
decidedly more fuel efficient. The bottom line was that the prototype diesel transfer locomotive could haul more tonnage, use
less fuel, and require substantially less maintenance than the
existing fleet of Mikados.

The success of EJ&E's prototype DT-6-6-2000 model led
Baldwin to produce 45 more of the type between 1948 and
1950. These later locomotives carried the same designation
and were rated the same but were powered by a pair of the turbocharged 606SC engines. It should be no surprise that EJ&E
was the largest customer for the model and ultimately acquired
25 of them.

After introduction in 1950 of its New Standard Line, Baldwin
offered an RT-624 transfer cab powered by a pair of 606A
engines. This was rated at 2,400 horsepower, which put it among
the most powerful freight units on the market. It was similar in
appearance to the DT-6-6-2000 but featured a more utilitarian
hood design. Most of the RT-624s used a drop-equalizer truck
instead of the cast-frame Commonwealth C truck favored on the
DT-6-6-2000s. Pennsylvania Railroad bought all but one of the
24 RT-624s. Baldwin RT-624 specifications indicate it was 74
feet, 10 inches inside couplers, and 15 feet, 4¼ inches tall over the
cab. It was 16 feet longer and slightly taller than Baldwin's AS-616
road-switcher. Lima-Hamilton offered a very similar type of
transfer locomotive for about a year, but Baldwin acquired Lima
in 1950 and discontinued Lima's locomotive line a year later. All
of Lima's transfer locomotives were sold to PRR.

EARLY ROAD DIESELS

The introduction of Electro-Motive's E-unit in 1937 established the diesel-electric as a fast passenger locomotive, while its model FT introduced the commercial diesel as a heavy freight hauler in 1939. These locomotives not only challenged the longstanding superiority of steam power in both fields and established the basic parameters emulated by most other builders in the coming years, but they enabled Electro-Motive to become the leading producer of locomotives in the following decades.

Initially, Baldwin took a divergent approach and engineered some very unusual diesel locomotives. Electro-Motive's philosophy was intended to assign multiple E-units (with and without cabs) in order to generate desired output, typically resulting in A-B-A or A-B/A-B-B locomotive consists to haul long streamlined trains. By contrast, beginning in 1940, Baldwin considered emulating conventional steam and electric locomotive practice. Instead of multiple diesel units, Baldwin planned to design a single unit that could match the

In an image dated February 1, 1949, Baldwin's 2,000-horsepower DT-6-6-2000 transfer-cab demonstrator passes a Union Switch & Signal lower-quadrant semaphore on Southern Pacific's Coast Line at milepost 309.7 near Arguello, California. Although SP didn't order this Baldwin model, its Cotton Belt subsidiary bought one in May 1948. *Baldwin image No. MG-199, Railroad Museum of Pennsylvania (PHMC)*

SPECIFICATIONS
Baldwin RT-624

Wheel arrangement: C-C

Engines: Two 606A diesels

Horsepower: 2,400

Total engine weight: 354,000 lbs.

Tractive effort: 88,500 lbs. (based on 25 percent adhesion)

Pennsylvania Railroad ordered all but one of the 24 RT-624 transfer locomotives built by Baldwin-Lima-Hamilton. Minneapolis & Northfield Southern took the one remaining unit. Even with this relatively small order for locomotives, PRR had three different variations. The locomotives came with two different types of trucks. Built in 1951, PRR No. 8952 features Commonwealth cast-frame C trucks, while others use a General Steel Castings fabricated, outside-equalized C truck. In addition, some PRR units were equipped with dynamic brakes, although No. 8953 was not. In general, this variation of the center-cab transfer locomotive was unusually short-lived.

Baldwin image No. 14205-4, construction No. 75123, courtesy H. L. Broadbelt Baldwin Collection (RR88.2), Railroad Museum of Pennsylvania (PHMC)

output of modern steam or electrics. It considered various wheel arrangements that mimicked those employed on the most powerful electrics of the day. Ultimately it settled on the 2-D+D-2 wheel arrangement, which was deemed suitable for high-speed passenger service and applicable for freight applications. While this may seem bizarre to modern eyes, it must be remembered that Baldwin and Westinghouse had built heavy electrics jointly using this arrangement on some big electrics for Great Northern. Since diesel-electrics were, in essence, an outgrowth of heavy electric technology, these arrangements seemed to Baldwin a natural advancement of existing locomotive technology, while offering a distinctly different approach than that of Electro-Motive.

Using a massive streamlined carbody 91 feet, 6 inches long and featuring a Spartan engineer's cab obviously inspired by those on Electro-Motive diesels and contemporary streamlined electrics, Baldwin planned for a "modular" locomotive that could accept up to eight compact diesel engines. Baldwin's plans for this leviathan were hampered by World War II. It was mid-1942 before the machine began to take shape. The prototype was a contemporary of the T1 Duplex experimental built for Pennsylvania Railroad.

Baldwin's road diesel was intended to use a new De La Vergne engine, designated model 408, rated at 750 horsepower. In the original configuration, with eight engines installed, the locomotive would generate 6,000 horsepower, deemed to be equivalent to a modern 4-8-4 in passenger service, thus the locomotive's road number: Baldwin Locomotive Works 6000. The machine was designed for 117-mile-per-hour operation, and by mid-1943 the beast was ready for testing. Although it reached 85 miles per hour on its debut run, serious design inadequacies resulted in an ignominious road failure that ultimately contributed to Baldwin canceling the project.

While this ended interest in a single-unit, modular, 6,000-horsepower diesel and effectively killed the prospects for the 408 diesel engine as locomotive propulsion, it wasn't the end of Baldwin's 2-D+D-2 wheel arrangement. A number of authors relate the story of Seaboard Air Line officials visiting Eddystone and being impressed by the potential of the massive experimental diesel's running gear, if not the modular diesel approach to propulsion.

With a potential customer at the gates, during 1945 Baldwin salvaged running gear from No. 6000 for use in a new locomotive. This emerged as Seaboard Air Line No. 4500, delivered to the railroad in December of that year. Except for the running gear, this was a completely new design, built to a revised approach and featuring a new carbody style and new prime movers and electrical gear, among other significant changes. It was the first locomotive to have the so-called "baby-face" cab, a more refined design with gentler curves than Baldwin 6000, yet still resembling Electro-Motive's automotive-inspired designs from the 1930s. In fact, it bore a remarkable similarity to the "bulldog" nose that debuted on Electro-Motive's FT in 1939.

Although this massive, multiwheeled machine was rated at just 3,000 horsepower (half the output of Baldwin's original concept), the company boasted of its creation in a brochure largely derived from an article in the February 1946 *Railway Mechanical Engineer*: "World's most powerful single-unit, diesel-electric [is] another example of Baldwin pioneering in the field of railway motive power. . . ."

The brochure goes on to detail every element of the new locomotive, a type variously classified in subsequent publications as model DR-12-8-3000 or DR-12-8-1500/2 but which has come to be commonly known as the "Baldwin Centipede" because of its long body and numerous wheels. Like No. 6000, the wheelbase was 77 feet, 10 inches long. The carbody measured 91 feet, 6 inches long and at its widest was 10 feet, 8 inches, while the top of the locomotive was 15 feet, 1 inches above the rail. Both the front and rear were tapered, so the back of the carbody was just 8 feet, 2 inches wide.

Seaboard intended to assign No. 4500 to high-priority "perishable" trains that carried fruits and vegetables from Florida to markets in the Northeast. Except for the initial Baldwin prototype, no other locomotive in diesel practice ever used such complicated running gear. The 16 driving wheels were powered by eight traction motors. This design was intended to provide maximum tractive effort and horsepower while keeping axle weight to a minimum. The maximum axle-loading on SAL 4500 was just 51,250 pounds—substantially less than that later employed by Baldwin's heavy road-switchers. The February 1946 *Railway Mechanical Engineer* explained, "additional traction motor capacity . . . makes it possible to absorb full engine horsepower at a speed of 72 mph."

Instead of the unreliable experimental 408 diesels used to power BLW 6000, SAL 4500 used a pair of Baldwin's new turbocharged, eight-cylinder 608SC engines, each generating 1,500 horsepower. This diesel was an advancement of the vertical inline VO engine that successfully powered Baldwin's World War II–era switchers. The engine had been redesigned in an effort to overcome earlier design flaws and limitations. The essential parameters, including bore and stroke, were retained. Among the changes was an improved cylinder-head configuration featuring vertically mounted fuel injectors and dual intake and exhaust ports on each cylinder. The flat-top piston used on the VO was replaced with a crowned design. Significantly, the hemispherical combustion chamber that had characterized the VO was discontinued, and the engine was designed to accept a turbo-supercharger that required a stronger crankcase. The

Completed on April 15, 1947, National Railways of Mexico No. 6400 was the first of the railroad's 14 Model DR-12-8-1500/2 SC Centipedes. Of the three railroads to operate this exceptional road diesel, NdeM maintained its models the longest, with some locomotives surviving into the early 1970s. It's a pity that none of this curious type was preserved. *Baldwin image No. 13611-4, construction No. 76672, courtesy H. L. Broadbelt Baldwin Collection (RR88.2), Railroad Museum of Pennsylvania (PHMC)*

application of the Elliott-Buchi turbocharger boosted output of the eight-cylinder engine by 50 percent—a substantial power increase. The February 1946 *Railway Mechanical Engineer* profiled the turbocharger:

[This] is a self-contained unit, comprising a gas turbine and a centrifugal blower mounted on a common shaft. The exhaust gas from the engine is conveyed to the Turbocharger [sic] through four pipes (two cylinders per pipe). The energy in the exhaust gas from the engine cylinders is used to drive the centrifugal blower, without demand on the power developed by the engine. The blower supplies all of the air required by the engine at a pressure a few pounds above atmospheric (approximately 5 to 6 lbs.).

Railway Mechanical Engineer continued its detailed explanation, noting, "The speed and output of the Turbocharger vary automatically and promptly with variations in load or speed, or both, of the engine. The Turbocharger operates at approximately 10,000 r.p.m. when the engine is operating at full load and full speed."

Both of the DR-12-8-3000's 1,500-horsepower 608SC engines were directly connected to separate Westinghouse 489-B main generators, which each powered one of two four-axle powered trucks. Each truck was equipped with four axle-hung Westinghouse-type 370 traction motors, one engaging each axle using reduction gearing. (The design of Baldwin No. 6000 intended for each 408 engine and generator to power an individual traction motor–axle combination.)

The locomotive weighed 577,200 pounds in full working order and placed 410,000 pounds on drivers. Using the 25:54 gear ratio, it delivered 123,000 pounds starting tractive effort (based on 30 percent adhesion) and had a continuous tractive effort rating at 20.5 miles per hour of 45,300 pounds. This was the most powerful single-unit diesel locomotive of its era. It would be two decades before any single locomotive unit would rival the Baldwin Centipede's power potential.

Ultimately, SAL ordered 14 of the type for freight services, delivered in 1947 and 1948. National Railways of Mexico bought another 14, initially for passenger services, although the Dolzalls note that these were rebuilt and upgraded by Baldwin in the mid-1950s and reassigned to freight work. Pennsylvania Railroad ordered the largest fleet, 24 units built during 1947 and 1948 and initially assigned in semipermanently coupled pairs to passenger services. These didn't fare well in long-distance work and after a few years were reassigned to freight service. Most finished out their days as helpers on Horseshoe Curve. An additional two Centipedes were ordered by Union Pacific, but this order was canceled and the two orphans were

SPECIFICATIONS
Baldwin DR-12-8-3000

Wheel arrangement: 2-D+D-2
Engines: Two Model 608SC diesels
Horsepower: 3,000 combined
Total engine weight: 577,200 lbs.
Tractive effort: 123,000 lbs. starting tractive effort (based on 30 percent adhesion with 25:54 gear ratio)

The first of Pennsylvania Railroad's Centipedes (known as model DR-12-8-3000 or DR-12-8-1500/2) pose for their official portraits at Eddystone. Baldwin's photographer made pictures at several angles of the enormous twin-engine diesels. Unlike Seaboard's Centipedes that were intended to operate singly in road-freight service, PRR's were semipermanently coupled and intended for fast passenger service. Later, they were reassigned freight duties. *Baldwin image No. 14674-3, construction No. 73131, courtesy H. L. Broadbelt Baldwin Collection (RR88.2), Railroad Museum of Pennsylvania (PHMC)*

painted as Baldwin demonstrators. Although these tested on the Baltimore & Ohio, Baldwin secured no additional DR-12-8-3000 orders. Ironically, the type was effectively obsolete before Baldwin completed its final steam locomotive orders and remains among the most unusual diesels to have ever worked North American rails.

ROAD PASSENGER DIESELS

Following the unsuccessful trials of Baldwin 6000, the company decided to pursue a path akin to that established by Electro-Motive's E-unit and developed a 2,000-horsepower carbody type powered by dual prime movers and riding on A1A trucks. In most respects, this was an E-unit clone using Baldwin-Westinghouse technology. A demonstrator, numbered BLW 2000, began to

take shape in 1944 and, upon completion, was put on tour in 1945. A second demo was built in 1945. Both were powered by Baldwin's proven eight-cylinder VO engine. After their tour, National Railways of Mexico bought the demo pair and ordered a third for passenger services. The demonstrators generated very little interest in the type, compared with the robust sales Electro-Motive was enjoying with its new model E7 at the same time. Interestingly, what few orders Baldwin received for its passenger diesel, known as model DR-6-4-2000, were for distinctive, custom-made machines—no two orders were identical.

Early-production DR-6-4-2000s used pairs of Baldwin's eight-cylinder 608NA engine. Only a handful of locomotives were so built: two for Gulf, Mobile & Ohio, and two three-unit orders for double-cab locomotives for Central Railroad

When Union Pacific canceled its order for Centipedes in 1948, Baldwin dressed the pair of DR-12-8-3000s (DR-12-8-1500/2s) in demonstrator paint and assigned them Nos. 6000A and 6000B to reflect their combined output. By this time, Baldwin's original 6000 had been scrapped and its running gear integrated into Seaboard Air Line No. 4500. We can only imagine how these big Baldwin diesels would have looked dressed in UP Armour Yellow. *Baldwin image No. 15377, construction Nos. 73129 and 73130, courtesy H. L. Broadbelt Baldwin Collection (RR88.2), Railroad Museum of Pennsylvania (PHMC)*

of New Jersey. Both featured the baby-face cab introduced on the Centipede. All of the company's later 2,000-horsepower locomotives were powered by pairs of the six-cylinder, turbocharged 606SC and styled by Raymond Loewy for Pennsylvania Railroad using an adaptation of the wedge-shaped "sharknose" design applied to the T1 Duplex steam engine. In addition, Baldwin built a unique single-606SC-powered, baby-face-cab unit for Chicago & North Western based on the DR-6-4-2000 that some sources designate as a DR-6-2-1000. This unusual machine featured only one powered truck, with the back half of the locomotive serving as a baggage compartment.

Baldwin also developed a 1,500-horsepower passenger type, model DR-6-4-1500, powered by a single 608SC and using A1A-style trucks. New York Central and Seaboard Air Line were the only customers. Production of the model, featuring the baby-face cab, totaled just nine units, including two cab-less boosters for NYC.

Excluding the Centipedes, Baldwin's total carbody-style passenger production from 1945 to 1948—including demos, double-enders, sharknoses, C&NW's hybrid, and the 1,500-horsepower models—accounted for just under 50 units. Electro-Motive's E7 production run in the same period topped 500 units and was succeeded by the E8 and E9 models, which accounted for another 600-plus units by 1964. Needless to say, Baldwin carbody passenger diesels were a rare breed, and the few sold generally didn't serve very long.

Gulf, Mobile & Ohio was one of the few railroads to test Baldwin's 1945-built, 2,000-horsepower demonstrator and then to follow up with orders. Still, GM&O was among Baldwin's smallest customers for passenger diesels and operated only a pair of DR-6-4-2000s. Chicago & North Western bought a similar unit, but this featured only one engine with the rear portion of the locomotive serving as a baggage compartment. *Courtesy Matt Gray Collection (RR95.2), Railroad Museum of Pennsylvania (PHMC)*

ROAD FREIGHT

Electro-Motive's four-unit FT freight diesel not only demonstrated the capabilities of diesel locomotives in heavy freight service but established the B-truck, multi-unit carbody diesel as the predominant type for heavy service. Over the next 15 years, Electro-Motive built thousands of "F-units," which were the driving force behind the rapid dieselization of American railroads. The success of the FT led other builders to emulate its format. After World War II, Baldwin introduced its own carbody freight diesels in the form of the DR-4-4-1500. These matched the output of Electro-Motive's units, and since Baldwin's initial production units used the baby-face cab, they bore an uncanny resemblance to Electro-Motive's Fs.

Like Baldwin's 1,500-horsepower road-switchers, its road freight diesels were powered by the eight-cylinder 608SC diesel. They were produced during 1947 and 1948 for Central Railroad of New Jersey, New York Central, and Missouri Pacific. In 1949, Pennsylvania Railroad ordered the model in the Loewy-styled sharknose body type. These distinctively Baldwin diesels remain among the most unusual-looking locomotives of the postwar period. In addition to PRR's order, Baldwin constructed a demonstrator set that notably toured on the Southern Pacific, demonstrating its abilities on that

SPECIFICATIONS

Baldwin DR-4-4-1500

Wheel arrangement: B-B

Engines: 608SC diesel

Horsepower: 1,500

Total engine weight: n/a

Tractive effort: n/a

Baldwin No. 6001 was a four-unit DR-4-4-1500 demonstrator set built in 1949. It traveled the United States in this livery to promote Baldwin road diesels. After the tour, the set was sold to Elgin, Joliet & Eastern, one of Baldwin's better early diesel customers. EJ&E, however, operated the quartet for a short time before reselling the set to Baltimore & Ohio. Photographs of these "sharks" in EJ&E's orange-and-green livery are exceptionally rare. *Baldwin image No. 15364-3, construction Nos. 73981, 73982, 73983, and 73984, courtesy H. L. Broadbelt Baldwin Collection (RR88.2), Railroad Museum of Pennsylvania (PHMC)*

railroad's sinuous and steeply graded Siskiyou Line. SP didn't buy the cab units but was a significant customer for Baldwin's road-switcher and switcher types. Elgin, Joliet & Eastern picked up the demo set and sold it to Baltimore & Ohio a few years later.

In 1950, Baldwin's New Standard Line offered the 1,600-horsepower, 608A-powered RF-16 model to replace the older road freight model. These were bought by established Baldwin cab-unit users New York Central, Pennsylvania Railroad, and Baltimore & Ohio, and all featured the sharknose body. RF-16s were noted for their slow-speed pulling ability, and most served in heavy freight service, typically working mineral trains in

western Pennsylvania, West Virginia, and Ohio. According to Baldwin's specifications, each RF-16 A-unit weighed 248,000 pounds fully loaded and, with the standard 15:68 gear ratio, delivered 73,800 pounds tractive starting effort (based on 30 percent adhesion). The continuous tractive effort rating (at 9.2 miles per hour) was 52,500 pounds. The locomotives were 15 feet tall, 10 feet, 6 inches wide, and 54 feet, 8 inches long (B-units were 18 inches shorter). All used the Westinghouse 471 main generator and four Westinghouse-type 370 traction motors. The RF-16 remained in production through 1953. Baldwin's domestic production of road freight carbody diesels totaled 265 units.

Similar to Baldwin's domestic road units were 51 R-616Es built for export to Argentina in 1953 and 1954. These six-motor units featured a variation of the sharknose carbody style. These Argentinean sharks would make for an interesting in-depth case study. Where the majority of domestic Baldwin carbody types were withdrawn from service in the mid-1960s, many Argentinean units survived into the 1980s. While domestic Baldwins tended to be viewed as curiosities and so didn't receive adequate or appropriate maintenance, when they were favored they tended to perform more reliably and survived much longer in service.

MECHYDRO 1000

Baldwin's final diesel production consisted of three low-profile, lightweight power cars called Mechhydro units assigned to experimental passenger trains tested by New Haven and New York Central in the mid-1950s. Known as model RP-200s, these were unlike all other Baldwin diesel units, not just because of their unusual B-2 wheel arrangement (trailing truck unpowered), but because they used distinctive technology licensed from Germany. They were powered by 1,000-horsepower Maybach diesels and featured diesel-hydraulic transmissions instead of the more common diesel-electric arrangement, thus the unusual

Beginning in 1949, Pennsylvania Railroad ordered Baldwin's Model DR-4-4-1500 in "sharknose" carbodies styled by Raymond Loewy that bore a resemblance to his steam T1 lines, rather than the "baby-face" carbody used by Central Railroad of New Jersey, Missouri Pacific, and New York Central. Mechanically and electrically the two styles were built to essentially the same specifications. Pictured here are Pennsylvania Railroad RF-16 sharks. Externally these locomotives were also very similar in appearance to PRR's DR-4-4-1500s. Among the primary internal differences was the RF-16's improved diesel engine—Model 608A rated at 1,600 horsepower and replaced the postwar 608SC engine rated at 1,500 horsepower. *Baldwin image No. 14103-5, construction Nos. 74819, 74820, and 74831, courtesy H. L. Broadbelt Baldwin Collection (RR88.2), Railroad Museum of Pennsylvania (PHMC)*

name. New York Central ordered one for its *Xplorer* train, while New Haven took a pair for service on a train styled the *Dan'l Webster*. All were out of service by the end of 1960.

ANOTHER SCENARIO

Baldwin's slow diesel developments in the 1930s have been attributed in part to the company's struggling finances (the company declared bankruptcy in 1935), as well as a prevailing belief by top management that, despite advances in diesel technology, steam locomotive technology still had a long and prosperous future. While Baldwin did move toward diesel development, it moved too slowly. It lost the advantage, and its actions tended to be reactive rather than progressive. It was Electro-Motive's moves in the diesel market that forced Baldwin to take a competitive outlook.

How would have Baldwin fared if the company had acted swiftly and decisively on Vauclain's cautionary intuition in 1926 and set about immediately in the development of high-output

Baldwin had long relied on export sales for a significant portion of its locomotive business. After World War II, it sold many diesels abroad. The final Baldwin-Lima-Hamilton export models were R-615Es sold to the Argentine State Railways in 1953 and 1954. No. 5001 was the first of the six-motor, broad gauge variation of the RF-16 road diesel. While most RF-16s ended service in the United States by the mid-1960s, some of the Argentinean R-615Es worked into the mid-1980s. *Baldwin image No. 14476-3, construction No. 75856, courtesy H. L. Broadbelt Baldwin Collection (RR88.2), Railroad Museum of Pennsylvania (PHMC)*

This conceptual drawing demonstrates the size difference between a conventional Baldwin diesel-electric and the low-profile, lightweight, Baldwin-built Mechydro diesel-hydraulic power cars built for New York Central and New Haven railroads. Each was powered by a German-built Maybach V-12 MD-655 diesel. New Haven's train, *Dan'l Webster*, was designed for power cars at both ends, while Central's *Xplorer* only required one power car. *Baldwin image No. 16709-42, courtesy H. L. Broadbelt Baldwin Collection (RR88.2), Railroad Museum of Pennsylvania (PHMC)*

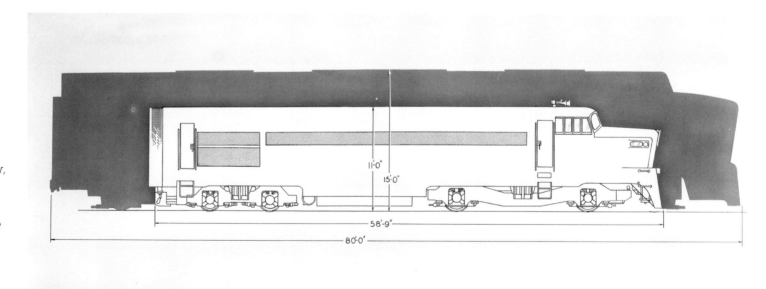

NEW YORK CENTRAL

An artist's impression of New York Central's *Explorer* (later *Xplorer*) along the Hudson Valley. Baldwin's ill-fated Mechydro power cars were its final domestic locomotive efforts. This low-profile, lightweight train (called Train-X in its conceptual phases) was the realization of Central's visionary chairman, Robert R. Young, who hoped to use modern trains to speed up schedules and operate more competitive passenger services. *Baldwin image No. 16709-07, courtesy H. L. Broadbclt Baldwin Collection (RR88.2), Railroad Museum of Pennsylvania (PHMC)*

diesel engines and diesel-electric locomotives? If by 1930 Baldwin had been experimenting with state-of-the-art diesel technology and by 1935 had refined this into the premier diesel technology of the day, would General Motors have bothered to make a substantial investment in the locomotive market? Perhaps Baldwin would have remained at the top of the locomotive business through the twentieth century and its diesels would still be working the rails today. We will never know.

Although decades have passed since Baldwin ended production, a few of its diesels have soldiered on. Nothing lasts forever, though. June 7, 2004, marked a solemn occasion near Sunnybrook, California, where Baldwin S-12 No. 10 made the final revenue run of the Amador Foothills Railroad. Efforts are underway to preserve this locomotive that was built in 1952 for Southern Pacific affiliate Texas & New Orleans. *Philip A. Brahms photo*

SOURCES

Books

Alexander, Edwin P. *Iron Horses*. New York: Bonanza Books, 1941.

———. *American Locomotives*. New York: Bonanza Books, 1950.

Alymer-Small, Sidney. *The Art of Railroading, Vol. VIII*. Chicago: Railway Publishing Society, 1908.

American Railroad Journal—1966. San Marino, Calif.: Golden West Books, 1965.

A Textbook on the Locomotive and the Airbrake. Scranton, Pa.: International Textbook Company, 1901.

Bell, J. Snowdon. *The Early Motive Power of the Baltimore and Ohio Railroad*. New York: Angus Sinclair Company, 1912.

Brown, John K. *The Baldwin Locomotive Works 1831–1915*. Baltimore, Md.: Johns Hopkins University Press, 1995.

Bruce, Alfred W. *The Steam Locomotive in America*. New York: Bonanza Books, 1952.

Bryant, Keith L. *History of the Atchison, Topeka and Santa Fe Railway*. Lincoln: University of Nebraska Press, 1974.

Bush, Donald, J. *The Streamlined Decade*. New York: George Braziller, 1975.

Churella, Albert J. *From Steam to Diesel*. Princeton, N.J.: Princeton University Press, 1998.

Conrad, J. David. *The Steam Locomotive Directory of North America, Vol. 1*. Polo, Ill.: Transportation Trails, 1988.

———. *The Steam Locomotive Directory of North America, Vol. 2*. Polo, Ill.: Transportation Trails, 1988.

Dolzall, Gary W., and Stephen F. Dolzall. *Diesels from Eddystone: The Story of Baldwin Diesel Locomotives*. Milwaukee, Wis.: Kalmbach Publishing Company, 1984.

Drury, George H. *Guide to North American Steam Locomotives*. Waukesha, Wis.: Kalmbach Publishing Company, 1993.

Forney, Matthias N. *Catechism of the Locomotive*. New York: The Railroad Gazette, 1876.

Garmany, John B. *Southern Pacific Dieselization*. Edmonds, Wash.: Pacific Fast Mail, 1985.

Harding, J. W., and Frank Williams. *Locomotive Valve Gears*. Scranton, Pa.: International Textbook Company, 1928.

Heck, Robert C. H. *The Steam-Engine and Other Steam-Motors, Vol. I*. New York: D. Van Nostrand, 1907.

Heimburger, Donald J. *Wabash*. River Forest, Ill.: Heimburger House, 1984.

History of the Baldwin Locomotive Works 1831–1923. Philadelphia: Bingham Company, 1923.

Kiefer, P. W. *A Practical Evaluation of Railroad Motive Power*. New York: Steam Locomotive Research Institute, 1948.

Kirkland, John F. *Dawn of the Diesel Age*. Pasadena, Calif.: Interurban Press, 1994.

———. *The Diesel Builders, Vol. I.* Glendale, Calif.: Interurban Press, 1985.

———. *The Diesel Builders, Vol. II.* Glendale, Calif.: Interurban Press, 1989.

———. *The Diesel Builders, Vol. III.* Glendale, Calif.: Interurban Press, 1994.

Kirkman, Marshall M. *The Compound Locomotive (1899).* Whitefish, Mont.: Kessinger Publishing, 2007.

Klein, Maury. *Union Pacific, Vol. I.* New York: Doubleday, 1989.

———. *Union Pacific, Vol. II.* Garden City, N.J.: Doubleday, 1990.

Kratville, William, and Harold E. Ranks. *Motive Power of the Union Pacific.* Omaha, Neb.: Barnhart Press, 1958.

Marre, Louis A. *Diesel Locomotives: The First 50 Years.* Waukesha, Wis.: Kalmbach Publishing Company, 1995.

Marre, Louis A., and Jerry A. Pinkepank. *The Contemporary Diesel Spotter's Guide.* Milwaukee, Wis.: Kalmbach Publishing Company, 1985.

Middleton, William D. *When the Steam Railroads Electrified.* Milwaukee, Wis: Kalmbach Publishing Company, 1974.

Newhall, Beaumont. *The History of Photography.* New York: Bulfinch, 1964.

Peabody, Cecil H. *Thermodynamics of the Steam-Engine and Other Heat-Engines.* New York: John Wiley & Sons, 1901.

Pinkepank, Jerry A. *The Second Diesel Spotter's Guide.* Milwaukee, Wis: Kalmbach Publishing Company, 1973.

Ransome-Wallis, P. *The Concise Encyclopedia of World Railway Locomotives.* New York: Hawthorn Books, 1959.

Reck, Franklin M. *The Dilworth Story.* New York: McGraw-Hill, 1954.

———. *On Time.* LaGrange, Ill.: Electro-Motive Division of General Motors, 1948.

Rosenblum, Naomi. *A World History of Photography.* New York: Abbeville Press, 1984.

Signor, John R. *Donner Pass: Southern Pacific's Sierra Crossing.* San Marino, Calif.: Golden West Books, 1985.

———. *Tehachapi.* San Marino, Calif.: Golden West Books, 1983.

Simmons, Jack, Ed. *Rail 150: The Stockton & Darlington Railway and What Followed.* London: Taylor & Francis, 1975.

Sinclair, Angus. *Development of the Locomotive Engine.* New York: Angus Sinclair Publishing, 1907.

Snell, J. B. *Early Railways.* London: Octopus Books, 1972.

Solomon, Brian. *Alco Locomotives.* Minneapolis, Minn.: Voyageur Press, 2009.

———. *The American Diesel Locomotive.* Osceola, Wis.: MBI Publishing Company, 2000.

———. *The American Steam Locomotive.* Osceola, Wis.: MBI Publishing Company, 1998.

———. *EMD Locomotives.* St. Paul, Minn.: MBI Publishing Company, 2006.

———. *GE Locomotives.* St. Paul, Minn.: MBI Publishing Company, 2003.

———. *Locomotive.* St. Paul, Minn.: MBI Publishing Company, 2001.

———. *Steam Power.* Minneapolis, Minn.: Voyageur Press, 2009.

———. *Super Steam Locomotives.* Osceola, Wis.: MBI Publishing Company, 2000.

Staufer, Alvin F. *Pennsy Power III.* Medina, Ohio: Alvin F. Staufer, 1993.

———. *Steam Power of the New York Central System, Vol. 1.* Medina, Ohio: Staufer Books & Prints, 1961.

Staufer, Alvin F., and Edward L. May. *New York Central's Later Power 1910–1968.* Medina, Ohio: Alvin F. Staufer, 1981,

Steinbrenner, Richard T. *The American Locomotive Company: A Centennial Remembrance.* Warren, N.J.: On-Track Publishers, 2003.

Stretton, Clement E. *The Development of the Locomotive: A Popular History 1803–1896.* London: Bracken Books, 1896.

Swengel, Frank M. *The American Steam Locomotive, Vol. 1, Evolution.* Davenport, Iowa: Midwest Rail Publications, 1967.

Swingle, Calvin F. *Modern American Railway Practice, Vol. VII.* Chicago: National Institute of Practical Mechanics, 1908.

Taber, Thomas Townsend III. *The Delaware, Lackawanna & Western Railroad, Part One.* Muncy, Pa.: Thomas Townsend Taber III, 1980.

Vauclain, Samuel M. *Optimism*. Philadelphia: privately published, 1924.

Vauclain, Samuel M., with Earl Chapin May. *Steaming Up!* New York: Brewer & Warren, 1930.

Vauclain Compound Locomotives, Cross-Compound Locomotives, Tandem and Balanced. Scranton, Pa.: International Textbook Company, 1905.

Westing, Frederick. *The Locomotives That Baldwin Built*. Seattle, Wash.: Superior Publishing Company, 1966.

White, John H. Jr. *American Locomotives: An Engineering History 1830–1880*. Baltimore, Md.: Johns Hopkins University, 1968.

———. *Early American Locomotives*. New York: Dover, 1972.

Wiswessar, Edward H. *Steam Locomotives of the Reading and P&R Railroads*. Sykeville, Md.: Greenberg Publishing, 1988.

Papers and Original Manuscripts

Johnson, Ralph P., chief engineer. *The Four Cylinder Duplex Locomotive as Built for the Pennsylvania Railroad*. Presented in New York, May 1945. Published in Philadelphia, Pa.

———. *Railroad Motive Power Trends*. Presented November 1945. Published in Philadelphia, Pa.

Meyer, C. W. *Comments on Ralph P. Johnson's Paper, November 29, 1945*. Presented November 1945. Published in Philadelphia, Pa.

Robertson, Donald B., and Alan Hegler. *BLW Construction List 1833–1956, CN 1-76,149*. Menlo Park, Calif., 2003.

Warner, Paul T. *The Baldwin Classification System*. Philadelphia, Pa., 1940.

———. *Compound Locomotives*. Presented in New York, April 14, 1939.

———. *The Story of the Baldwin Locomotive Works*. Philadelphia, Pa., 1935.

———. Untitled notes on Philadelphia & Reading steam locomotives. 1939.

U.S. Patents

Baldwin, Matthias W. No. 2759, "Manner of Constructing Locomotive Steam-Engines by which they Adapt Themselves to the Curves and Undulations of the Road." August 25, 1842.

Brochures, Timetables, and Company Documents

Baldwin Locomotive Works. *6,000 H.P. Diesel Electric Road Freight Locomotives*. Philadelphia, Pa., 1949.

———. *Baldwin Diesel-Electric Switching Locomotives Operator's Manual. No. DS-100. Diesel-Electric Passenger Locomotive*. Philadelphia, Pa., 1947.

———. *Baldwin Diesel-Electric Switching Locomotives Operator's Manual. No. DS-103. 660-1000-1500 hp Switchers and Road Switchers*. Philadelphia, Pa., 1947.

———. *Baldwin-Westinghouse Diesel-Electric Locomotives General Specifications for Standard Units*. Philadelphia, Pa., 1950.

———. *Catalogue of Locomotive Details*. J. B. Lippincott & Company, 1885.

———. *Eight-Coupled Locomotives for Freight Service. Record No. 99*. Philadelphia, Pa., 1920.

———. *Exhibit at the Panama-Pacific International Exposition, San Francisco, Calif., 1915*. Philadelphia, Pa., 1915.

———. *The Fifty-Thousandth Locomotive. Record No. 92*. Philadelphia, Pa., 1918.

———. *The Forty-Thousandth Locomotive*. Philadelphia, Pa., 1913.

———. *Illustrated Catalogue of Locomotives*. J. B. Lippincott & Company, 1881.

———. *Locomotive Number 60,000 an Experimental Locomotive*. Philadelphia, Pa., 1926.

———. *Logging Locomotives. Record No. 76*. Philadelphia, Pa., 1913.

———. *Steam Locomotive Performance*. Philadelphia, Pa., 1940.

———. *Recent Development of the Locomotive. Record No. 73.* Philadelphia, Pa., 1912.

———. *Triple Articulated Compound Locomotive for the Erie Railroad Company. Record No. 81.* Philadelphia, Pa., 1915.

Jersey Central Lines. *Diesel Electric Locomotives.* Jersey City, N.J., 1953.

Philadelphia & Reading Railway Company. *Motive Power & Rolling Equipment Details.* Reading, Pa., circa 1899.

———. *Report of the Philadelphia and Reading Rail Road Company with Accompanying Documents.* Philadelphia, Pa., 1839.

Baldwin Archives

Baldwin Locomotive Works Negative Log Index No. 1 1870–1906.

Baldwin Locomotive Works Negative Log Index No. 2 1905–1913.

Baldwin Locomotive Works Negative Log Index No. 3 1913–1918.

Baldwin Locomotive Works Negative Log Index No. 4 1918–1925.

Baldwin Locomotive Works Negative Log Index No. 5 1926–1954.

Baldwin Locomotive Works Register of Engines Vol. 1. 1833–1902.

Baldwin Locomotive Works Register of Engines Vol. 2. 1902–1913.

Baldwin Locomotive Works Register of Engines Vol. 3. 40000–60000 (1913–1927).

Baldwin Locomotive Works Register of Engines Vol. 3. 60000–80000 (1927–1956).

Baldwin Locomotive Works, *Photograph Schedules* [nd].

Letter to R. P. Johnson from R. Vezin on the Pennsylvania Railroad S-2 Turbine, May 14, 1945.

Periodicals

Baldwin Locomotives. Philadelphia, Pa. (no longer published).

Diesel Era. Halifax, Pa.

Diesel Railway Traction (supplement to *Railway Gazette* UK; merged into *Railway Gazette*).

Extra 2200 South. Cincinnati, Ohio.

Jane's World Railways. London.

Milepost. Friends of the Railroad Museum: Strasburg, Pa.

Official Guide to the Railways. New York.

Pacific RailNews. Waukesha, Wis. (no longer published).

Proceedings of the New England Railroad Club 1897–1898. Springfield, Mass.

Railroad History (formerly *Railway and Locomotive Historical Society Bulletin*). Boston.

Railway Age. Chicago and New York.

Railway and Locomotive Engineering. New York (no longer published).

Railway Mechanical Engineer. (no longer published).

TRAINS Magazine. Waukesha, Wis.

Vintage Rails. Waukesha, Wis. (no longer published).

INDEX